ITALO BALBO'S FLIGHT
TO THE
1933 CHICAGO
WORLD'S FAIR

ITALO BALBO'S FLIGHT
TO THE
1933 CHICAGO
WORLD'S FAIR

DON FIORE

THE
History
PRESS

Published by The History Press
Charleston, SC
www.historypress.com

First published 2023

Manufactured in the United States

ISBN 9781467155342

Library of Congress Control Number: 2023940783

CONTENTS

INTRODUCTION

In his iconic tribute to Chicago, Carl Sandburg spoke of the city's perpetually restless energy, building, tearing down and building anew; its many neighborhoods forever locked in transitional cycles; industrial giving way to residential and destitution to gentrification—all under the backdrop of a constantly evolving downtown skyline. Even the course and directional flow of its river were changed. Stagnation has never been part of Chicago's lexicon.

But it's also a city filled with public artwork and monuments that, once erected, were usually expected to remain in place, integrated permanently into the surrounding landscape. Some have risen to landmark status—the two equestrian warriors that flank Congress Parkway, for instance, or Millennium Park's reflective kidney bean–shaped *Cloud Gate*, having expanded their role to instantly identifiable emblems of Chicago.

Yet even these are subject to the turbulent, roiling flow of change that forever courses across the years. Civil unrest following the death of George Floyd while being taken violently into custody by Minneapolis police rapidly expanded from demands for law enforcement reforms to a comprehensive, national reexamination of virtually every component in American society. In education, entertainment, business and even the English language itself, assessments have been made and changes proposed or enacted—sometimes moderately, other times radically—with the goal of excising what some believe to be problematic components from American society that reflect or are actually rooted in real or perceived racial or gender inequities.

In 2020, Chicago's civic monuments, like others across the country, unavoidably became part of the discussion after several of them—including statues of George Washington, Abraham Lincoln, William McKinley and Christopher Columbus—were vandalized and damaged by those who believe them to be symbols of oppression and racism.

In response to this, then mayor Lori Lightfoot created the Chicago Monuments Project, a commission made up of academicians, artists and community representatives that, after conducting a wholescale study of the city's commemorative public artwork and memorials, identified and recommended the removal or modification of those works that, in the group's opinion, no longer resonate positively with modern sensibilities. The CMP was also tasked with suggesting replacement monuments that were more inclusive and reflective of the city's diverse racial and ethnic profile.

No one cognizant of the prevailing trends could be surprised by the conclusions transmitted in the final report which the CMP submitted to Lightfoot in 2022, or which monuments appeared at the top of hit list. Two of them, an ancient Roman column and a bronze statue of Columbus, both echoes from Chicago's A Century of Progress World's Fair, relate directly to the subject of this book. A third municipal tribute, a street name, joins these monuments to complete the last, tangible vestiges of honors bestowed on a foreign visitor named General Italo Balbo. Although he was the city's guest for a brief handful of days, his achievements and presence impressed Chicagoans on such a towering scale that they were compelled to pay permanent homage through the durability of concrete, bronze and marble. It is this author's belief that the residents of the Chicago metropolitan region should at least be familiar with the story behind these extraordinary tributes before their final fate is determined. This work will hopefully lend itself toward that objective.

I wish to thank my old friend and colleague Commendatore Robert Allegrini, whose unfailing encouragement and support helped make this project possible, as well as so many others who assisted me along the way. Special gratitude is extended to Professor Dominic Candeloro, curator of the Italian Cultural Center in Stone Park, Illinois; Paul Basile, editor of the Italian American monthly magazine *Fra Noi*; Professor Gregory Alegi, aerospace journalist and author; General Maurizio Cantiello, Italian air attaché at Washington, D.C.; and Frank Di Piero, Martin Caliendo and Kristina Gordon White.

I am further indebted to my loving wife and life partner, Rene; my daughter, Victoria; and my son, DJ, for their encouragement, suggestions and, above all, their patience and understanding through this lengthy project. Finally, this effort is dedicated to the memory of my father, Antonino Rocco Fiore, from whom I first learned of the subject of this book in my childhood.

RELICS FROM 1933 ALONG THE LAKEFRONT

Though Balbo Drive is one of the shortest stretches of pavement depicted on a Chicago street map, its prime location, running east and west between State Street and DuSable Lake Shore Drive at the southeast edge of the Loop, has made it well known to the thousands of motorists who cruise past it every day. Radio listeners across the metro area know its name from its frequent references in traffic reports.

It's highly probable that the overwhelming majority don't know or really care whom the street commemorates. Those who do pay notice may well assume that it's a misspelled tribute to the sixteenth-century Spanish explorer Vasco de Balboa.

In the sprawling, well-manicured acres of lakefront park land a few blocks south of the street, a weathered Corinthian-style Roman column juts up an imposing eighteen feet on an eroding and fissured base. Two inscriptions, one in Italian and one in English, tell its story, though now barely legible after years of exposure to Lake Michigan's punishing winter winds.

At the nearby corner of Columbus Drive and Roosevelt Road, a bronze statue of Christopher Columbus once towered in heroic pose on an equally towering base. The statue was removed by the city after being badly vandalized by protestors during the civil unrest that erupted across the nation in the wake of the death of George Floyd. But the statue's granite base remains, amply embellished with allegorical figures, symbols and engraved tributes, one of which bears the same name of the above-referenced street—the name by which the Roman column monument is also officially known.

That name is embroidered into the tiniest patch of Chicago's vast cultural and historical tapestry. The three civic tributes bearing it have been standing essentially as insignificant, visual white noise in the city's consciousness for three quarters of a century. Normally.

With almost predictable regularity, someone—a politician, a reporter, a university professor—will make a serendipitous discovery of the actual identity of the man honored by the tributes. Controversy will flare up over the subsequent weeks, with outraged letters, editorials and petitions to the Chicago City Council or Park District demanding the column be removed, the street name changed or both (the comparatively oblique tribute on the Columbus monument is usually overlooked). Within weeks, though, interest will wane, the topic will cease being discussed on radio talk shows and the angry letters to the editor will stop coming in. The tributes will slip back into tranquil and unmolested anonymity. The name Balbo—whether unnoticed, disparaged, honored or ignored—clings tenaciously to its place in a small corner of Chicago history.

Like so much of the surrounding landscape and structures in the area where the tributes are concentrated, their presence is a direct consequence of the Century of Progress World's Fair, a spectacular two-year international exposition that opened on May 27, 1933, in the midst of the Great Depression.

With millions of jobless Americans still seeking their daily sustenance in breadlines and soup kitchens, it hardly seemed a proper time to throw a party. Yet the dazzling neon and Art Deco wonderland that arose on Chicago's lakefront provided the nation with a sorely needed spiritual uplift as it struggled through those gloomy years.

Although the fair was scheduled to mark the one hundredth anniversary of Chicago's municipal incorporation, its underlying message paid little attention to the past. Prosperity, though remote, could be at least envisioned along the shores of Lake Michigan, where spellbinding images of a better tomorrow came to life within the brightly illuminated exhibition halls that lined the Burnham Park fairgrounds. In an era of fear and doubt, the Century of Progress shouted its exuberant message of confidence in the future through the miracles of science and technology.

For this very reason, no foreign nation was better represented at the fair than Italy. Approaching its eleventh year in power, and still on friendly terms with the Western democracies, Benito Mussolini's government was eager to showcase the economic and technological progress it had brought to the Italian kingdom. Visitors to the eye-catching, prominently placed Italian pavilion, the Hall of Sciences and other fairground structures encountered a vast array of exhibits in which dioramas, newsreels, charts and photos displayed the vibrancy of Mussolini's new Italy. Highlighting impressive feats of civil engineering and massive public works projects like the draining of the Pontine Marshes, the expansion of railroads, electrical distribution networks and the construction of highways, the exhibits were of keen interest to Americans. In the not-so-distant future, their own government under the Roosevelt administration would launch similar infrastructure projects on a colossal scale to employ millions and help pull the nation out of its economic malaise.

The Century of Progress, of course, was not Chicago's first world's fair. Forty years earlier, the city had hosted the World's Columbian Exposition, farther down on the Lake Michigan shoreline on reclaimed swamp land that is now Jackson Park. Distinguished by its symmetrically perfect classical architecture and staid sense of propriety, that earlier event looked to the past in a celebration of Western civilization's scientific and cultural achievements since the arrival of Columbus to the Americas in 1492, whereas the 1933 fair locked its vision firmly on the future. But for Italy, a tragic factor played a role in distinguishing the two expositions.

In 1891, eleven Italian nationals, including a fourteen-year-old boy, had just been acquitted for the murder of a local sheriff when they were nonetheless rounded up and executed by a New Orleans mob in what would be the largest mass lynching in American history. The Royal Italian Government protested immediately, demanding that the perpetrators of this atrocity be brought to justice and that indemnities be paid to the families of the victims. When these demands were rejected at both state and federal levels, the Italian kingdom broke off diplomatic relations with the United States. Tensions heightened, and it was rumored that the Royal Italian Navy, at the time larger and more formidable than its American counterpart, was steaming to the Gulf of Mexico on a punitive mission to bombard New Orleans. Although nothing so dramatic occurred, the possibility of war between the two nations, if not probable, at least appeared possible.

At the very same time the crisis was unfolding, plans for the Columbian Exposition were already intensely in process, and every major nation across the globe was sketching out the extent and nature of its participation. Owing to the bitter dispute with the United States, however, Italy withdrew itself from the fair's international planning board.

Eventually, the American government relented and agreed to pay a $25,000 indemnity to each of the murdered men's families. Diplomatic relations were restored, but it was far too late for Italy to participate in the world's fair in anything more than a token way. Therefore, while Great Britain, France, Germany and every other prominent power were represented by great, architecturally elaborate national pavilions to proudly display their histories, achievements and products, Italy's presence was close to nonexistent.

The year 1933 offered the country a second chance to stand up and be counted at a new Chicago world's fair, and the Italians seized the opportunity with unequaled enthusiasm and vigor. The year 1933 also happened to mark the tenth anniversary of the founding of the *Regia Aeronautica*, the Royal Italian Air Force, a fact that lent itself to the modern, up-to-the-minute image that Italy was striving to project. Of all the developing technologies, none evoked a more exciting vision of the future than aviation, and any nation's level of power and prestige could be measured with some accuracy by its level of activity in this burgeoning field. It was no coincidence, then, that the architectural lines of the fair's Italian pavilion clearly suggested the geometrics of an aircraft.

When the topic turned to aeronautics, however, the Italians didn't plan to stop at diagrams, charts and displays. They intended to present the real thing. A sensation was caused, then, when Italy announced that it would highlight its participation at the fair by sending a fleet of two dozen seaplanes on a transatlantic flight to Chicago.

Since getting a single aircraft safely over the ocean was still a considerable challenge—of the eighty-five recorded attempts thus far, only twenty-eight had been successful—completing the journey with an entire squadron was a first-of-its-kind proposition, one that would require planning and organization on an unprecedented scale. But there were few doubts among those who kept abreast of aeronautical developments that the Italians were up to the task, particularly since it would be executed by the young General Italo Balbo, in whose confident and robust hands the Royal Italian Air Ministry had been placed in 1926.

ITALIAN PROMINENCE IN EARLY AVIATION

Since the 1940s, popular American imagination rarely, if ever, places Italy among the leading nations that guided aviation through its formative years. That prestigious list is usually reserved for the United States, Great Britain and France. In truth, however, the Italians were at the forefront of every aspect of aeronautics and universally recognized and respected as such during its early stages of development.

A mere five years after the Wright brothers and Kitty Hawk, the Kingdom of Italy became the first nation in history to successfully deploy airplanes on the battlefield while fighting the Turks in Libya. Setting up airbases in the outskirts of Tripoli and Benghazi, they pioneered every modern wartime use of aircraft except air-to-air combat and troop transport. They would certainly have pioneered those fields had their opponents possessed planes and had aircraft with greater load capabilities been available. They were the first to use planes to experiment with aerial reconnaissance, topographical mapmaking using aerial photography, artillery spotting and even assault when Lieutenant Giulio Gavotti lobbed hand grenades on enemy troops from his aircraft while flying reconnaissance on November 7, 1911. Foreign news correspondents covering the war duly reported these activities and helped convince their respective nations of the role air power would play in the future.

The Italian victory in 1912 further destabilized the already troubled Turkish Ottoman empire, particularly in the Balkans, and it was in that very region where the First World War would erupt two years later. The

Italian military aviators during the 1911 Italo-Turkish War. *Author's collection.*

commencement of hostilities shoved military aviation out of its infancy, with each of the major combatants establishing its own air corps. Here, too, Italy took the lead in several areas, especially in long-range strategic and tactical bombing by sending squadrons of giant Caproni triplanes over the Adriatic to blast enemy ports and rail yards.

Though victorious in the war, the Kingdom of Italy found itself buried in unimaginable debt, and the transition to a peacetime economy proved clumsy and difficult. Many new industries had been founded to respond to wartime needs in a country that only a few years earlier had traded chiefly in agriculture. When government contracts were abruptly canceled after the Armistice, those industries, lacking peacetime functions to return to, were forced to lay off vast numbers of workers. Their suddenly idle ranks faced the grim prospect of being joined by some 3 million demobilized soldiers returning to civilian life and looking for jobs.

The nation's aircraft production, negligible when Italy joined the conflict in 1915, ballooned enormously during the war, increasing to one hundred new planes per week. Production lines were shut down with the cessation of hostilities, but the War Ministry was still left with a vast surplus inventory that it could no longer afford to maintain.

A strategy was devised to sell the planes to countries that had not developed their own aeronautical industries. By opening new foreign markets for their products, the burgeoning Italian aircraft manufacturers could hopefully survive the threat of financial ruin.

A series of long-distance flights or "goodwill missions" were launched to points across Europe, usually attempting to set a new record or aeronautical milestone in the process. Always piloted by young but seasoned wartime veterans, these flights met with some success, as the governments of several Scandinavian and eastern European nations wrote out purchase orders for Italian aircraft as a result. Planes were even shipped to South America, where Antonio Locatelli, another veteran pilot, utilized an Ansaldo SVA, a gracefully agile but sturdy biplane developed by the Italians during the war, to complete the first round-trip flight over the Andes.

The biggest attention grabber, however, took place in the summer of 1920, when Lieutenants Arturo Ferrarin and Guido Masiero each completed a twenty-five-thousand-mile aerial odyssey from Rome to Tokyo in two SVAs. A half million Japanese were on hand to greet the Italians, and their achievement was publicly celebrated for a solid month, during which every conceivable accolade and honor was showered upon them. The Ferrarin-Masiero feat served as the inspiration and catalyst of ever more impressive ventures in succeeding years.

Arturo Ferrarin in Tokyo. *From* Il Mio Volo Roma *(1921).*

For the time being, though, postwar Italy was plunged into political and economic chaos, a situation that fueled the growth and increasing influence of the newly formed Fascist Party—its ranks filled with military veterans who were furious that their battlefield sacrifices had brought scarce tangible benefits to their country or themselves. The Italian Socialist Party and other movements on the left also emerged as forces to be reckoned with, and violent demonstrations and clashes between the supporters of the two ideologically opposing parties were common occurrences across the entire peninsula.

In October 1922, the Fascists threatened to forcibly seize control of the country by mobilizing tens of thousands of their black-shirted ranks on a march to Rome. King Vittorio Emanuele III, Italy's reigning monarch, was advised to call out the army to confront the Fascists. Fearing an outright civil war, he instead invited party leader Benito Mussolini to the royal palace for a conference, which concluded with Mussolini's appointment to the office of prime minister.

This didn't mean that the Fascists suddenly gained full control of the government. When forming his cabinet, Mussolini named members of multiple parties to head the various ministries, and parliament was still composed of representatives from across the political spectrum. This would continue until 1925, when he maneuvered to dissolve all other parties and assumed dictatorial powers (although the king always retained his position as head of state).

By then, the economy was regaining its footing after the postwar turmoil, and political dissension was actively suppressed. Facing no possible opposition, Mussolini's goal of transforming Italy into a first-tier world power proceeded unhindered.

These were the times when nothing elevated a nation's status more than its aeronautical capabilities, and the reorganization and advancement of that sector was a priority. Just one year after Mussolini's ascension to head of government, the *Regia Aeronautica*, or Royal Italian Air Force, was created to become the world's second independent military air arm, preceded only by Britain's Royal Air Force. A national commissariat for aeronautics and later an actual air ministry were incorporated into the government to regulate and promote civil and commercial aviation, along with re-stimulating the growth of the aircraft manufacturing sector and its many satellite industries.

Fascist party lieutenant Aldo Finzi, a veteran wartime ace from an old Italian Jewish family, took charge of the *Regia Aeronautica* and the commissariat, only to be forced to resign after being linked to several public scandals. He was replaced by the politically neutral army general Alberto Bonzani, whose limited aeronautical experience was outweighed by his excellent reputation as a focused and competent administrator. Bonzani must have known that the position was temporary since he habitually showed up to work in his army uniform. But his diligence brought the structural and financial order to Italy's aeronautical sector, and this stabilization allowed Mussolini to feel confident enough to restore its control to Fascist hands. In November 1926, Bonzani was replaced by the robust thirty-year-old Italo Balbo.

ITALO BALBO AND THE *REGIA AERONAUTICA*

talo Balbo was born in Ferrara on July 5, 1896, the son of a schoolteacher. His family's comfortable middle-class home was furnished with well-stocked shelves of history, science and geography books, as well as the popular adventure novels by Verne, Defoe and Dumas, all of which he and his three siblings were actively encouraged to read. As he entered his teens, Balbo had absorbed enough to start forming his own political philosophy, strongly favoring the fervent republicanism of the nineteenth-century Italian revolutionary Giuseppe Mazzini, in direct opposition to his father's staunch support of the Italian monarchy.

Mazzini, an ardent champion of Italian unification and independence, persisted in adhering to the vision of his country as a democratic republic even after the united Kingdom of Italy came into existence in 1861. But one belief shared by both republicans and monarchists was that the nation's unification would never be truly complete until all Italian-populated regions outside the national borders were incorporated into the country, a major part of which were under the control of the powerful Austro-Hungarian empire.

Reclamation of these so-called unredeemed territories was the overriding motive behind Italy's eventual involvement in World War I. When the conflict broke out in 1914, furious debate over whether or not to join the fight raged throughout the country, with the political left demanding that Italy sit out the war and focus its resources on its many internal woes. Balbo, now in his late teens, roused more than ever with Mazzinian passion, threw

himself on the interventionist side, and when
Italy officially entered the conflict in 1915, he
lost no time enlisting in the army.

With Balbo attached to the Alpine divisions,
a section of the Royal Italian Army that
specialized in mountain warfare, it wasn't until
late in the war, during the strenuous battles at
Monte Grappa, that he saw the most action.
His calm performance under the most perilous
conditions elevated him to the rank of lieutenant
with one bronze and two silver medals on his
tunic by the time of the Armistice.

Balbo, like thousands of others, was not
discharged immediately after the war. The
government was metering demobilization to
avoid further increasing the already staggering number of unemployed
civilians. Still in uniform, he spent the early postwar months directing
army crews in the repair of war-damaged roads and bridges. After that,
he enrolled in university, obtained a political science degree, married and
started a family.

Italo Balbo during World War
I. *From* Eroi Alati *(1943).*

Though never renouncing his devotion to Mazzini's republicanism, Balbo
drifted toward the new, if loosely organized and vaguely defined, Fascist
movement. Its war-hardened adherents were bound by mutual contempt
toward the Socialists, whom they believed had undermined the war effort
and, through frequent, often violent strikes, disruptive public demonstrations
and factory and corporate farm takeovers, were sabotaging the country's
postwar recovery. This in itself, the veterans seethed, was a vicious insult to
the blood they and their companions had so recently shed on the battlefields.

On the other hand, the economic hardships suffered by much of the
population that the left sought to remediate were very real and continued
unabated, with neither the royal ministries nor a much-divided parliament
apparently capable of providing relief. Inflation was out of control. The cost
of housing and food soared while incomes dropped. All of this, of course,
strengthened the appeal of the Socialist and newly forming Communist
platforms that Italian history still records the immediate postwar era as the
biennio rosso (two red years).

By 1921, the scattered cells of "fasci" had begun to coalesce into an actual
political party, with Benito Mussolini—a veteran, journalist and former
Socialist himself—becoming its principal spokesman. Balbo, who by then

had returned to civilian life and was the leader of the Fascist cell in Ferrara, was not far behind.

Elements of the varying political leanings of the party's leadership, such as Mussolini's former Socialist background and Balbo's republican ideals, found their way into the Fascist platform. Labor reforms, an eight-hour workday, social safety nets for the elderly and disabled and compulsory education to move children from the workforce to the classroom were prominent components. But the party's bedrock tenet was nationalism. From corporate boardrooms to the wheat fields, it was every citizen's primary duty to devote his or her energies to the welfare and benefit of the state.

Although they didn't always find the social reforms easy to digest, wealthy landowners and industrialists appreciated the Fascist tenet of the sanctity of private property and enterprise and were soon sending checks in the party's direction. So-called Action Squads, militant gangs of black-shirted Fascists armed with cudgels and blackjacks, brutally dispersed striking workers, intimidated labor leaders and punished leftist enemies through their most infamously common practice of forcing them to drink a quart of castor oil.

As a "squadrista" captain, Balbo also participated in this dark business. An even uglier occurrence would emerge to cast a long-reaching shadow over him for decades. Balbo, along with Mussolini, Cesare De Vecchi and Emilio De Bono, became one of the four top Fascist leaders who organized the party's March on Rome in October 1922. Yet after King Vittorio Emanuele III appointed Mussolini to the office of prime minister as a result, Balbo was not given a cabinet position. Instead, he returned to his role as the party's leader in Ferrara and surrounding districts. Around that time, an activist Catholic priest named Giovanni Minzoni was busy promoting social and economic reforms quite independently of the Fascist platform. He even organized a popular youth group and was gaining so many followers so rapidly that the Fascists in the town of Argenta where the priest resided were alarmed. When their attempts to peacefully persuade Minzoni to desist with what they interpreted as anti-Fascist activities proved useless, they resorted to violence.

One night in August 1923, the activist priest and an associate were attacked by two squadristi, a scuffle that left the priest lifeless on the pavement with a fractured skull. Balbo was angered upon learning of the incident. With Mussolini in the prime minister's office, the Fascist hierarchy expected the rough-and-tumble days of the street brawling squadristi to fade into the past. Continuing acts of violence thwarted the party's attempts to win legitimacy and respectability as a serious, responsible political entity capable of bringing peace and prosperity to the much-troubled nation.

But here Balbo made a grievous mistake. The individual accompanying Minzoni on the fatal night survived the assault and was able to identify the perpetrators. Rather than allowing their arrest and letting justice take its course, Balbo tried to shield them from prosecution and attempted to persuade local newspapers to downplay the story. Instead, one of them, *La Voce Repubblicana*, ran an editorial accusing Balbo himself of having a hand in the murder.

Outraged, Balbo sued the paper for libel. At the subsequent court hearing, its editors clarified that Balbo, while not actually involved in the crime, was morally complicit by not keeping party underlings in line and allowing their most brutal practices to go unchecked. The court ruled in *La Voce*'s favor, the suit was dismissed and Balbo was ordered to assume the costs of the trial.

He resigned in humiliation from active party leadership and lowered his public profile. Sometime later, he turned his attention to the creation of a new, regional newspaper named *Corriere Padano*, which he published and edited. Although decidedly Fascist in content, the paper occasionally echoed Balbo's stubborn independence by running editorials criticizing some of the policies of Mussolini's own cabinet in Rome. Shortly thereafter, and clearly hoping to exert greater control over Balbo's renegade tendencies, Mussolini called him to Rome and named him undersecretary of the economy.

It was an odd appointment, since Balbo was no economist. But he took the job seriously enough by enlisting some of the country's most proficient fiscal experts as advisors. In any case, it was only a temporary role since Mussolini had already intended to transfer him to the Air Ministry as soon as the acting undersecretary Alberto Bonzani finished reorganizing the ministry after Finzi's brief tenure.

It was a perfect fit. Unlike the prosaic Bonzani, Balbo seized his position with palpable enthusiasm. Although not yet a pilot himself, he had always been enthralled by aviation, following its development closely in his youth. He applied for pilot training in the army's air division during the war, but to his disappointment, he was denied. The calamitous Austro-German breakthrough at Caporetto in 1917 triggered the mustering of every available man to hold back the rapidly advancing enemy, and he was sent back to the front.

Now, however, there was nothing to stop him from learning how to fly, and after a one-month crash course, he was finally awarded a pilot's license. While he would never hone his skills beyond those of a competent but ordinary pilot, Balbo at least was one of the few aviation chiefs in the world who actually knew how to fly a plane.

Under Bonzani, the *Regia Aeronautica* was largely purged of the glaringly Fascist character that Finzi had infused in it. Balbo, at least for the present, prudently left many of these changes undisturbed since his predecessor's handling of all other aspects of the job had produced positive results. He found himself presiding over an already bustling field on the first day he stepped into the Air Ministry office.

The Italian aviation industry was making a promising comeback, with no less than a dozen major, privately owned aircraft companies once again engaged in active production. A national weather service agency was established under the aviation commissariat, which boasted the most up-to-date technologies and meteorological equipment. The year 1926 also saw Italy's first commercial airlines begin operations, with four separate companies offering regular routes between the nation's major cities and, by August, service to Athens, Istanbul and the Italian-occupied island of Rhodes. Airmindedness was visible almost everywhere. Even the Italian Post Office, under the Ministry of Communications, was issuing the world's first airmail stamps. In fact, the Italians were sporadically experimenting with handling the country's mail distribution by air as far back as 1911, but in April 1926, permanent national airmail service went into operation.

After a lull, the far-flung goodwill flights of the postwar years began making a comeback. On November 7, 1925, almost one year to the day prior to Balbo's appointment as undersecretary of aviation, a well-weathered seaplane touched down on the brown, slow-moving waters of the Tiber, its pilot greeted like a victorious Caesar returning from his conquests amid the wildly cheering citizens of Rome. Colonel Francesco De Pinedo of the *Regia Aeronautica* had just successfully completed a spectacular seven-month aeronautical tour-de-force across the Eastern Hemisphere, logging thirty-four thousand miles from Italy to Japan and back, circumnavigating Australia along the way. Sponsored by the *Regia Aeronautica*, the goodwill mission took De Pinedo and his flight companion, mechanic Ernesto Campanelli, to a dozen countries in their Savoia-Marchetti S-16 biplane, with the international press covering every step of their journey.

Italy was a regular, leading competitor at the Schneider Trophy Races, an annual international speed contest in which seaplanes raced against the clock on an offshore course hosted by whichever country had won the previous year. The 1926 edition, held at Hampton Road, Virginia, ended with the Italian team claiming its third official (and fourth technical) victory after the Macchi M-39 flown by Mario De Bernardi completed the 217-mile

De Pinedo with the S-16 biplane used in his 1925 Asian tour. *Italian Air Force Historical Office.*

course at an average speed of 246 miles per hour, winning the trophy and setting a new world record for seaplanes.

Six months before De Bernardi's astounding performance, and thousands of miles away in an infinitely less hospitable environment, a massive airship plied its way majestically through the cloud-laden sky above the Arctic Ocean, its destination the North Pole. Known as the Amundsen-Ellsworth-Nobile Expedition after its three principal participants, the international venture combined the regional expertise of Norwegian polar explorer Roald Amundsen, the funding of American millionaire Lincoln Ellsworth and the aeronautical skills of Colonel Umberto Nobile of the *Regia Aeronautica*.

The airship, christened the *Norge*, was a semi-rigid dirigible, a type designed and perfected by Italian engineers at the *Stabilimento di Costruzioni Aeronautiche* (SCA), a state-run research and development facility for lighter-than-air equipment. More aerodynamic and maneuverable than other designs, semi-rigid airships were considered safer since lift was obtained through multiple, individual hydrogen-filled cells. The ship would remain airborne even with a sizeable breach of its outer envelope.

Nobile was director of the SCA and personally designed the airship that was he was now confidently steering over the frigid Arctic. Its five-man Italian crew was supplemented, at Amundsen's insistence, by a contingent of Norwegians who, having no experience in lighter-than-air flight, had to have been trained for their jobs at the SCA in Rome. Though officially billed as a multinational project, then, the expedition was solidly in Italian hands.

Fifteen hours after departing the Kings Bay in the Svalbard islands north of Norway, the airship crossed over the North Pole at 1:30 a.m. on May 12, 1926, at which point Norwegian, American and Italian flags were solemnly released to flutter down to the icy surface. The *Norge* then proceeded on to Teller, Alaska, where it terminated history's first flight across the Arctic Ocean. The airship was disassembled and shipped back to Italy, while the various participants, divided by nationality, embarked on a celebratory tour across the United States.

On the chilly, predawn morning of February 13, 1927, the irrepressible Colonel Francesco De Pinedo and a crew of two embarked on another spectacular aerial tour, this time of the Western Hemisphere, which would include a round-trip Atlantic crossing and set numerous aviation milestones. The three Italians would be the first to fly over the Brazilian rainforests, and when they touched down in New Orleans on March 29, their plane, a Savoia-Marchetti S-55 christened the *Santa Maria*, became the first foreign aircraft to fly to the United States on its own power.

De Pinedo's 29,180-mile goodwill tour of the Americas seized the world's attention, only to be wiped off the front page by Charles Lindberg's successful flight to Paris while the Italians were in Newfoundland, preparing their own return flight over the Atlantic. Despite this cruel act of fate, De Pinedo's historical achievements did not pass unrecognized. The U.S. Congress presented him with the Flying Cross, an award rarely given to foreign aviators, and the British decorated him with their equivalent medal.

Back in Italy, De Pinedo was promoted to general and conferred with the title of marquis by the king. Balbo politely applauded and praised the aviator, even giving him the sobriquet of the "Master of Distance." But

Francesco De Pinedo. *Italian Air Force Historical Office.*

he was determined to see that this latest solo performance would be De Pinedo's last. This was not based on personal disdain, although the two men nurtured a genuine dislike of each other, but on Balbo's conviction that, at least in Italian aviation, the day of the individual diva was over.

De Pinedo was quietly absorbed back into the bureaucratic framework of the *Regia Aeronautica*, assigned, at least temporarily, to the desk and file cabinet world of an administrative position. Although he was already in office at the time it began, Balbo was forced to allow De Pinedo's tour to proceed, since it had already been planned, budgeted and announced. Now, however, he was making it clear that the government would not support any future flights that involved a single aircraft. The *Regia Aeronautica* would still sponsor goodwill tours, but all such voyages would be henceforth conducted by whole squadrons of planes to more closely reflect Italy's growing military strength and unity of purpose.

Fate itself assisted Balbo in grounding Umberto Nobile, another so-called aeronautical diva. Also having been promoted to general after his successful arctic flight, Nobile had planned a second aerial expedition to the North Pole, but this time as an exclusively Italian enterprise. Again, Nobile's international popularity prevented Balbo from interfering with these plans, although he did withhold financing. Instead, the expedition was funded by the Royal Italian Geographical Society and private subscriptions, with additional assistance provided by the Royal Italian Navy. The airship, again designed by Nobile himself, was proudly christened the *Italia*, and with an eighteen-man crew, it began making its way to the Arctic Circle on April 15, 1928.

With Kings Bay Norwegian Island of Spitsbergen as base, the plan was to make three flights, each into different Arctic zones, to collect geophysical and meteorological data, take magnetic measurements and conduct similar scientific research. The final venture would be to the North Pole, where for a second time the Italian flag would be dropped. The first two penetrations into the frigid Arctic skies were completed successfully, with the *Italia* logging more than three thousand miles over the ice. But on its return journey from the pole, the airship was literally torn to pieces by a ferocious Arctic storm, leaving its captain and surviving crewmen stranded on the ice packs for weeks before they could be located and rescued.

As with De Pinedo, Balbo and Nobile did not get along well, not so much for personal reasons but because the undersecretary saw no future in dirigibles. The tragic end of the *Italia*, in which many lives were lost both in the crash and in rescue attempts, allowed Balbo to rest his case. The SCA was shuttered, and Nobile, dismissed from the service, went off to teach lighter-than-air flight theory at an American college.

Even as Nobile was lifting off from Kings Bay, Balbo was in the midst of executing the first demonstration of his new vision for the *Regia Aeronautica* by means of leading a mass formation flight to Spain involving a remarkable sixty-one seaplanes. For this he relied heavily on De Pinedo, now universally recognized among the most seasoned and skilled aviators in the world, to organize and command this goodwill mission. When plans for the flight were reported by the foreign press, in fact, it was more often treated as the latest of De Pinedo's famous feats, with the then less familiar Balbo barely mentioned.

THE MASS FLIGHT PROGRAMS

De Pinedo was an unshakeable believer in the future of seaplanes and one of their most avid proponents of the era. With their country's nearly five thousand miles of coastline, most airminded Italians shared his faith in maritime aviation, and during the post-Armistice years, Italian manufacturers, aviation enthusiasts and the *Regia Aeronautica* itself tended to favor seaplanes. When Balbo's mass flight to Spain was proposed, the type of aircraft with which it would be executed was never debated.

Relieved at the chance to get back in the air and applying all of the lessons and precautions learned from his earlier aerial journeys, De Pinedo mapped out a 1,750-mile steppingstone route over the Western Mediterranean, with stops at Elmas (Sardegna), Pollensa (Mallorca) and finally various ports of call along the Spanish coast and southern France before returning to home base. These stopping points were chosen for having harbors or bays of sufficient size to accommodate the gargantuan sixty-one-plane fleet, and each locale was staffed in advance by a managing station officer, crews of mechanics, technicians, radio operators and other specialists. De Pinedo arranged for fuel and oil, spare parts and all other necessities to be on hand for use as needed at each port, as well as lodging and provisions for the 180 participants. As an additional safety measure, he requested and received the assistance of the Royal Italian Navy (*Regia Marina*), which dispatched two ships to

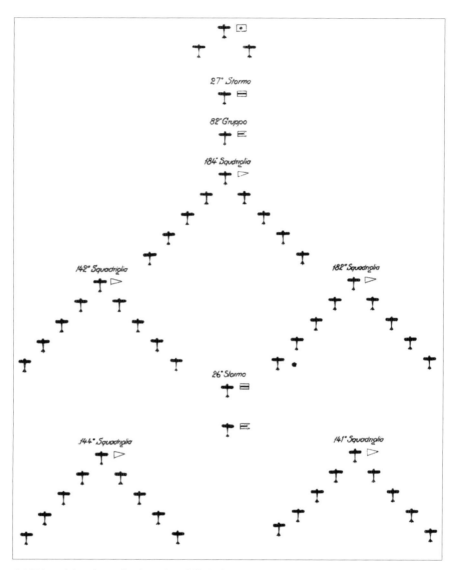

A 1929 aerial cruise to Spain order of flight formation. *From* Cieli E Mari *(1973).*

patrol the planned route for rescue action in the event of a mishap and to transmit weather conditions that awaited the flyers.

The formation outline consisted of a lead plane manned by De Pinedo and copilot Captain Ruggero Bonomi, followed by two "storms" (groups), each composed of twenty-five Savoia S.59 *bis* seaplanes, an updated version of the same design used by De Pinedo himself on his Asian-Australian tour three years earlier. One in an impressive catalogue of products by Italy's innovative aircraft builder SIAI Savoia-Marchetti, the durable flying boat was powered by an Isotta Fraschini 510-horsepower engine.

Following these squadrons were nine, larger Savoia S.55 flying boats, carrying additional support staff, journalists and various Italian officials, and a CANT.2 commercial plane with the Spanish, French, American and British air attachés as passengers. Fully aware that he was far surpassed in experience and skill by De Pinedo and most of the other pilots of the main squadron, Balbo was content to relegate himself to the cockpit of one of the rear-guard S.55s.

The launching point would be the aerodrome established during World War I by the *Regia Marina*'s aviation division at the town of Orbatello on the southern Tuscan shoreline, one hundred miles north of Rome. A strategic military stronghold since the time of the Etruscans, it occupies a narrow promontory thrusting into tranquil landlocked lagoons, well sheltered from the waves and currents of the Tyrrhenian Sea. Placed under control of the *Regia Aeronautica* in 1925, the locale was being expanded and developed as Italy's principal maritime aviation training and proving center.

Takeoff began at 6:20 a.m. on May 25, 1928, with De Pinedo's plane first in the air, falling back and circling above so the commander could observe each of the squadrons lift off in turn before taking its place at the head of the massive ensemble. Assuming diamond-shaped formations, the planes proceeded along the planned route and, to the astonishment of onlookers, descended and departed in flawless order at each itinerary point.

It was a sight never before witnessed—the sky thick with planes, an aeronautical flotilla approaching in unison, precisely spaced from one another, the air vibrating from the combined deep, rhythmic throb of their powerful engines.

The fleet anchored at the Spanish port of Los Alcazares on May 27, and the following day, a squadron of Spanish planes flew Balbo and his staff to Madrid, where a banquet in his honor was hosted by King Carlos and his family, while De Pinedo was left behind in custody of the planes and crews. After three more days of celebration, the cruise began its return course, first with a flyover above Marseilles and then docking at the port of Berre, France's largest seaplane base. The commanders and crews disembarked to attend a parade and banquet in their honor, and the celebrations intensified when news arrived that *Regia Aeronautica* pilots Captain Arturo Ferrarin and Major Carlo Del Prete were on their way to shattering the

Arrival in Spain. Balbo is fifth from right; De Pinedo second from right. *From* Cieli E Mari *(1973)*.

world records for speed, distance and endurance in a closed-circuit flight with a newly designed a Savoia S.64 monoplane.

The Western Mediterranean tour concluded on June 2, with the entire flotilla soaring over Rome in geometric formations and then circling north and descending on the blue lagoons at Orbatello, where they were welcomed home by Mussolini and thousands of spectators. Though hailed as the achievement's originator, Balbo characteristically deferred credit to De Pinedo, telling reporters, "Those of you who participated in the cruise saw firsthand the perfection that unfolded, not only by the planes in flight, but also at all of the bases. This is the result of the minute and intricate preparations executed by General De Pinedo and the men he selected to carry it out. Indeed, this cruise, so painstakingly organized and carried out flawlessly from start to finish, has revealed De Pinedo in a new light, no less important than that which has made him famous the world over. He is no longer just a great achiever of records and the conqueror of air paths around the globe, but also a leader, a General of greater capabilities than words can express. I cannot praise him highly enough."

From a practical standpoint, the route and bases carved out by the tour were soon developed for commercial air service between Italy and Spain, but its chief accomplishments, besides providing a blueprint for future mass flights, was turning the world's attention once more toward the rapid progress of Italian aviation.

Shortly thereafter, this achievement was complemented by a second mass flight in the opposite direction, eastward to the Black Sea and the Soviet Union. Assigned once again to the planning and execution of the enterprise, De Pinedo sketched out an itinerary that included stopovers in Greece, Turkey and Bulgaria before reaching the Ukrainian port of Odessa, the journey's ultimate destination. The return flight would be essentially the same, except for switching the Bulgaria stop to one in Romania. Selecting the landing points proved considerably more difficult than the flight to Spain, since Soviet and Turkish officials placed strict restrictions on which portions of their respective countries the aviators would be allowed to visit or even fly over.

The entire cruise would rack up greater mileage than its predecessor, so to keep expenses down, the number of participating aircraft was reduced to thirty-five. The bulk of the group was composed of S-55s, each with four-man crews, along with two S-59s and a Cant-22 for the civilian participants, chiefly journalists and members of the diplomatic corps.

Outside of that, the logistics closely mirrored those of the earlier cruise. Support staffs were dispatched to Athens, Varna (Bulgaria), Constanta (Romania), Istanbul and, of course, Odessa, the stopping points on the finalized route. Refueling and maintenance stations were set up, and the *Regia Marina* prepared to disperse a string of support ships along the route.

The Eastern Mediterranean cruise had the additional purpose of expanding sales of Italian planes to the countries en route. Except for the Soviet Union, the ports of call were in nations that lacked aeronautical industries and therefore were potential customers. Certainly the inclusion of the Soviet Union, the political antithesis of Fascist Italy, among the destinations seems curious. However, despite their vast ideological differences, the two nations maintained diplomatic relations, and the Soviets had been purchasing Italian aircraft for years.

On May 28, with all arrangements in place, the flying boats, staggered into groups, began departing from Orbatello to the port of Taranto on the heel of the Italian peninsula, the official starting point of the journey. There, after final inspections were performed, the Eastern Mediterranean cruise was launched on June 5 when the first band of planes lifted off in formation at 3:45 a.m.

The Italians were welcomed with predictable enthusiasm at each of the scheduled points of call, with the cheers and applause of the massive throngs greeting their alighting airplanes as they touched down in perfect formation. When the various heads of state and government of each visited country were not actually present at the landing site, Balbo, De Pinedo and the other high-ranking officers and participants were ceremoniously transported to meet with them.

But upon arriving at Odessa on June 8, the Italians were quick to note the absence of the festive ambiance and the usual mass of civilians who were always on hand elsewhere to cheer their arrivals. In fact, the port had been declared temporarily off limits to the public, with armed sentries stationed at every access point.

Balbo and his officers were received cordially by Soviet officials and transported by motorcade to two hotels that had been modernized and refurnished specifically for the occasion. Restrictions were loosened outside the port, and clusters of the city's inhabitants looked on, curious but eerily silent as the aviators were escorted to their lodgings.

After the usual string of celebratory banquets that followed, all characterized by mutual protestations of goodwill between the two nations, De Pinedo was invited to inspect and pilot a Soviet aircraft. This was reciprocated by allowing the Soviets to examine the Italian planes, a shrewd decision that resulted in a purchase order from Moscow for thirty-five S-55s.

Besides paying commercial dividends, the Eastern Mediterranean was another public relations triumph for exposing Italy's blossoming aeronautical capabilities and the top-notch equipment deployed to reach them. However, during its execution, the growing irritability between Balbo and De Pinedo became openly visible. Once back in Italy, the long-suppressed vitriol exploded. The two men bickered almost continually along the way, their differences exasperated by widely divergent personalities. De Pinedo, while by no means cold or aloof, was by nature reserved, taciturn, serious and focused. Imbued with the spit-and-polish traditions of the Royal Italian Navy from his years in the academy, he was a stickler for neatness, order and propriety. Balbo, on the other hand, was no career officer who had diligently worked his way up the ranks like De Pinedo. His rise to prominence was rooted in politics and activism and propelled by his own outgoing, assertive character.

Each brought his cases against the other to Mussolini, in De Pinedo's instance rather guilelessly. The matter came down to which of the two men, with their differing visions and contrasting personalities, would determine the course of Italian aviation. As Balbo put it, there was only room for one of them in that cockpit. Mussolini, of course, sided with his old Fascist Party stalwart, and De Pinedo was sent out of the country to serve as air attaché at the Italian embassy in Buenos Aires.

THE SOUTH ATLANTIC CROSSING

Toward the end of 1929, to commemorate the twenty-fifth anniversary of the Wright brothers' first successful flight at Kitty Hawk, North Carolina, President Coolidge and the U.S. Congress hosted the three-day International Civil Aeronautics Conference in Washington, D.C. Attended by more than four hundred delegates, roughly a quarter of whom were from thirty-nine foreign nations, the proceedings addressed aviation's role in international commerce, the standardization of aircraft industrial terminology and communication systems and a lengthy agenda of shared technical and logistical concerns.

Representing Italy, Balbo and aircraft builder Gianni Caproni were invited to speak at the conference, and with a delegation of other officials and Italian airline executives, they set sail for America in late November. Upon arrival, they joined other participants in an informal prelude to the proceedings that included a visit to an aircraft exposition in Chicago and a visit to the Dayton, Ohio home and workshop of Orville Wright, the surviving brother of the celebrated inventors. Greeted by reporters, Balbo eulogized the brothers and their historic achievements but missed much of the following day's ceremonies, retreating to his hotel room with a cold and a fever.

After a night's rest, he had recovered well enough to rejoin the delegation on a train for Washington, D.C., where he was scheduled to give one of the opening presentations for the conference. Reporting on the progress of commercial aviation in Italy, Balbo referenced the continuing expansion of routes and networks and the improvements in equipment, but most of all, he noted the importance of the safety of civilian passengers, a consideration that would be clearly reflected in his later deeds.

By this time, of course, Balbo's squadrista activities during the violent unrest of the early postwar years seemed like ancient history. The times had changed and so had he, maturing into a world-class leader in his field, well liked and respected by his peers at home and abroad. But among others, not so much. One month before Balbo's arrival, anarchist Carlo Tresca, who since immigrating to the United States in 1904 had risen to national prominence as a tireless labor organizer and journalist, was already planning to protest his presence on American soil. He used his newspaper, *Il Martello* (*The Hammer*), to remind the Italian American community that Balbo had the blood of the murdered priest Don Minzoni on his hands. When the conference got underway, Tresca and his followers and allies repeated the allegation in public demonstrations.

If any of this phased the Italian air minister in the least, he wasn't showing it. In fact, when confronted with protestors exhorting onlookers to join the radical movement, he chuckled and replied that he'd think about it.

But Balbo's American hosts harbored little tolerance for radicals. The 1920s had begun with one of the country's most notorious "Red Scare" episodes, and residual apprehension toward leftist activism lingered on. Only two years prior before the aviation conference, the Italian-born anarchists Nicola Sacco and Bartolomeo Vanzetti were executed in Boston, convicted of murder on the weakest of evidence and sentenced by an unabashedly prejudiced judge who openly referred to them as "anarchist bastards." American authorities regarded Tresca with no less disdain, and his attempts to dog Balbo for the duration of his visit placed him under close police surveillance. The U.S. Postal Service even refused delivery of all copies of *Il Martello* that labeled Balbo an outright murderer.

None of this had any effect on the conference, which, after concluding with a day trip to Kitty Hawk, saw most of the foreign delegates return to their respective homelands. Balbo, who had been joined by his wife, stayed on and embarked on a tour of the United States, albeit with a somewhat unusual itinerary.

Instead of heading for the normal tourist destinations, Balbo and his wife met with Henry Ford in Detroit, who gave them a tour of his factory. They subsequently visited U.S. Army and Navy aviation facilities in Pensacola,

San Antonio and San Diego, where he was invited to climb into the cockpit of an American plane and fly it to Los Angeles.

His firsthand exposure to American industrial and military strength impressed him profoundly, and he went home resolved to apply as much as practical of what he had seen to the direction of Italian aviation, along with the determination to return to the United States by air in the not-too-distant future.

Ideally, that goal would be achieved ideally in another formation flight, something believed to be outside the current technological capabilities of any nation. Executed flawlessly under De Pinedo's insistence on scrupulous preparation and focus on the most minute details, the Mediterranean cruises served as a logistical guidebook for future, more geographically ambitious mass flights. But a transatlantic attempt would naturally impose unique and untested challenges for an entire squadron. With the United States still in the corner of his eye, Balbo decided on a preliminary test in the form of a mass air cruise to Brazil.

Except for the number of planes involved, no new air paths needed to be opened, since that path had been blazed back in 1922 by the Portuguese aviators G. Coutinho and S. Cabral, who struggled their way from Lisbon to Rio de Janeiro in a trouble-plagued journey that took two and a half months and a series of aircraft replacements to complete. Five years later, De Pinedo and his crew kicked off their milestone tour of the Americas by tracing the same basic route, which began on the African and cut a sharp southwest angle into the Western Hemisphere. Not long after, De Pinedo's copilot, Carlo Del Prete, and Arturo Ferrarin, hero of the 1920 Rome-Tokyo flight, who had since become a team of record breakers, set a new world's nonstop long-distance record by completing the 4,400-mile shot from Italy to Brazil in forty-nine hours and nineteen minutes.

In fact, six out of the eight attempted crossings of the South Atlantic to that date had ended successfully (compared to a mere nine out of thirty-nine attempts over the North Atlantic). Still the formation flight concept was new and untested across any ocean, and it presented its own, unique problems to be surmounted. With De Pinedo out of the picture, planning and direction of the proposed crossing was assigned to Lieutenant Colonel Umberto Maddalena, a first-line pilot who had led a mission to locate and drop survival supplies to the *Italia* airship crew trapped on the desolate Arctic ice in 1928.

With some minor alterations, the proven flight path would be taken, but with the advantages of the comprehensive preparation and support infrastructure devised for the Mediterranean cruises. Two bases, essentially pit stops, would be set up at points along the West African coast, the final point at the island of Bolama off Guinea-Bissau (then called Portuguese Guinea). From there, one dozen S-55s would make the 1,875-mile leap over the ocean to Natal, Brazil.

The planes, all S-55s, were divided into groups of three, each group distinguished by the black, green, white and red markings on their hulls. The individual planes were further identified by the first four letters of their pilots' names painted in bold black letters on the underside of the wings, a system that would be duplicated in the North Atlantic cruise.

The *Regia Marina* furnished a fleet of eight ships to be distributed along the route, ready to assist in the event of a downed plane. A twelfth support vessel, an agile yacht christened *Alice*, was also put to hard work. Originally built for Monaco's ruling Grimaldi family, the ship had changed ownership and purposes over time, ranging from cargo carrier to military gunboat. At the time of the South Atlantic cruise, it was the property of the Italian airline company *Societá Anomina Navigazione Aerea* (SANA), utilized to transport materials and supplies to landing points that were part of its expanding service network on the African coast. As a vessel familiar to those waters, the *Alice* was leased by the Air Ministry to provide lodging for the air fleet crews, while also serving as a mess hall and radio and meteorological station. It was on the yacht that Balbo and his aviators enjoyed Christmas dinner, as they made their way toward Bolama during the final week of December 1930.

As De Pinedo and other South Atlantic flyers had learned, it was best to schedule takeoff after sunset, when cooler temperatures lessened the risk of overheated engines under the brutally scorching African sun. The power plants were already burdened with the heavy fuel loads needed to make the nonstop journey, and excessive ambient heat pushed them to the limit. The commencement of the flight, therefore, began under partially moonlit skies at 1:30 a.m. on January 5, 1931. The planes would take to the sky in groups of three and proceed forward on the route, with the following groups expected to catch up and fall into formation in sequence.

Twelve minutes after the last group began straining to leave the water, one of them spontaneously exploded, its remnants dropping like confetti into the sea. Another plane, struggling in its ascent, scraped awkwardly against the waves and tipped over, killing its mechanic. Rescue ships hurried to the site and retrieved the survivors and the bodies of the dead,

South Atlantic crossing. *From* Cieli E Mari *(1973)*.

but the remains of Captain Luigi Boer, the pilot of the fire-obliterated flying boat, were never found.

A third incident occurred when, after nine hours of flight, another aircraft was forced down to the water with a burst radiator and out-of-balance rear propellor. One of the navy patrol ships reached the plane to assist with on-site repairs, but when choppy waves made that impossible, the only option was to tow it to Fernando di Noronha island, 220 miles off the Brazilian coast. In attempting that task, a mishap with the towing chains caused one of the hulls to twist and partially detach from the plane. As the hull filled with water, the operation was aborted and the aircraft was allowed to sink. A forth aircraft, again forced down by an overtaxed cooling system, was retrieved and safely towed to the island, where it was repaired, refueled and took off successfully to link up with the fleet a few days later.

Meanwhile, the remaining planes successfully reached their destination after a total of eighteen nonstop hours at varying speeds and altitudes along the way. While undoubtedly a remarkable victory, the deaths of five participants naturally dampened the unbridled elation that would have otherwise marked the flight's conclusion. Balbo had been advised that two of his planes had ditched at the beginning of the flight but didn't learn the details until he had reached South America. He and his companions had been hoping to land to news that their crews had been safely retrieved and were alive and well.

Devastated upon learning of the death toll, he gathered his aviators together and informed them of the tragedies: "The price of our triumph brings with it terrible anguish, but also casts a sacred halo. The heroic death of our comrades testifies before the world the difficulties of our enterprise. Their martyrdom has magnified it. When we left Orbatello, we all knew that such a fate might claim any of us."

As a tribute, he rededicated the remaining planes in the fleet in honor of the fallen airmen, with each one's name inscribed on five of the flying boats. After inspections and minor repairs, the squadron flew to Bahia and finally to Rio de Janeiro, where a grand celebration was held for days. At that point, the planes were transferred to the Brazilian government, and Balbo and his aviators sailed home to Italy. Not long after their return, and with the permission of Portugal, the Air Ministry had an imposing granite monument erected at Bolama honoring the five casualties of the enterprise.

A few months later, the International Aviation Federation (FAI) awarded Balbo its gold medal for the year's most outstanding aeronautical accomplishment. Having earlier been promoted by Mussolini from undersecretary of aviation to air minister, he found himself elevated to a significantly higher tier of worldwide recognition. With these and the South Atlantic crossing under his belt, he was able to preside over his own international aviation conference at Rome in May 1932. This weeklong event, known as the Congress of Transoceanic Flyers and officially sponsored by the Royal Aero Club of Italy, brought together more than fifty aviators from around the world who had completed or at least credibly attempted flights across the Atlantic or Pacific Oceans to share their experiences in the specific difficulties encountered in meeting the challenge, as well as solutions through which those problems were or could be overcome.

Political and legal considerations were also on high the agenda, particularly regarding the standardization of air routes over international waters, the freedom of flight paths across national boundaries and open access to landing points in foreign countries. Like the 1928 conference in Washington, D.C., the overriding objective was the eventual establishment of routine commercial air lines between the continents.

Balbo came out hard in favor of the feasibility of regular transoceanic air service if international cooperation and protocols, such as the required sharing of meteorological data with flights in progress, could be reached. Most of the participants agreed except, curiously, the French delegation, which insisted on the right of exclusivity to certain ports of call. In any case, this was all a purely academic argument since, according to French aviator

Jean Assolant, regular transoceanic flights were impossible due to the distances involved, unpredictable weather and technological limitations.

Balbo, however, had done his homework. He insisted that regular intercontinental commercial air service on the South Atlantic route could be established immediately and produced minutely researched data to prove it. He detailed the requirements down to the aircraft type, range and speed, as well as infrastructure requirements, and concluded that an airline operating one round-trip flight per week could operate profitably with revenues from passenger, mail and cargo transport. Within a few years, Italian, German and French companies were indeed operating regular postal and shipping routes from Europe to South America by way of the West African coastal route, although regularly scheduled passenger service would not be available for several years.

The shorter and less precarious South Atlantic crossing, though, was of lesser interest to representatives from the United States and Britain, who were naturally more concerned with flight paths at higher latitudes. But the North Atlantic was also very much on Balbo's mind, with the groundwork for the flight to Chicago already in progress. In this connection, he was especially keen to hear what one of the delegates, the German aviator Wolfgang Von Gronau, had to say about his experiences. Von Gronau had been testing flight paths across the Atlantic at high northern latitudes, precisely the region that Balbo and his staff were considering for their own transatlantic cruise. While these shortened the distance between the hemispheres, they were also fraught with greater obstacles and challenges, not the least being sudden formation of impenetrable fog, frigid temperatures, iced wings, snow and freezing rain and few opportunities for an emergency landing. Even a seaplane's advantage of landing on the water also involved contending with icebergs and punishing waves. An airman's chances of surviving a flight over these regions, Von Gronau warned, depended on the amount and reliability of current and forecasted weather available to him.

Balbo took the advice seriously. He kept in touch with Von Gronau after the conference adjourned, and a long-lasting friendship developed, with Balbo even writing the introduction for a book the German flyer would later author on his own aeronautical exploits. Von Gronau later put Balbo in touch with the German meteorological specialists who had assisted him in his aerial explorations. It was a timely introduction, since plans for the *Regia Aeronautica*'s anticipated North Atlantic crossing were already taking shape.

At first, the possibility of a global flight was placed on the table. A preliminary committee was appointed to explore that idea, with some officers traveling as far as the Aleutians to explore potential landing sites and sketch out the most advantageous flight paths. Besides logistical difficulties, political considerations, specifically the Japanese invasion of Manchuria in 1931, discouraged venturing into that critical region of the globe, and the prospect was abandoned.

Instead, and on the advice of Mussolini, Balbo set the destination site of his next mass flight as Chicago and the world's fair. It was, in fact, the perfect choice, given the fair's forward-looking, central theme of scientific and technological progress where aviation played such an important part.

ITALY AND THE 1933 WORLD'S FAIR

When compared to Chicago's 1893 Columbian Exposition, foreign participation at the Century of Progress was conspicuously limited. With their economies battered by the global financial stress of the Great Depression, most nations opted out of the costly investment that involved constructing, staffing and maintaining an exhibition pavilion. The fair's organizers foresaw this and proposed the creation of a special section on the grounds called "Old Europe." The concept would relieve foreign governments of a great deal of expense by eliminating the need for large, individual national buildings. Instead, foreign countries would be represented through a cluster of small villages, where traditional cultural highlights of the respective nations would be featured.

The idea gained no traction. A primary purpose of any world's fair was to provide a venue for nations to advertise their products and strengthen trade, and the restricted space of the "villages" precluded the opportunity. But additionally, to many, the proposal invoked uncomfortable similarities to the 1893 fair's Midway, with its cheap re-creations of "exotic" foreign locales presented in the fashion of a circus sideshow. No foreign government was interested, and the European Village was scrapped. In the end, only a few nations built their own actual exhibition buildings, with some—like Great Britain, Canada and the Irish Free State—sharing space in the same structure. Other countries simply leased small sections in other fair halls for their displays.

To Italy's Fascist government, the Century of Progress presented a massive propaganda opportunity as much as or perhaps more than a commercial one, and it registered as a participant in September 1932. From there, Italy jumped in with both feet, leading it to become the most prominently represented foreign nation at the Century of Progress. The fair's official guidebook declared nothing short of this, telling readers, "The voice of modern Italy, vibrant with the heroic deeds of Fascism, speaks more resoundingly, more intelligently, and more forcefully to the World's Fair visitor than that of any other foreign nation participating in A Century of Progress."

The "voice" would emanate at clarion pitch from Italy's national pavilion, a sleek, concrete, metal and glass Art Moderne palace, and the central showpiece of the country's presence at the fair. Conceived by a team of the country's most innovative architects, its structural outline boldly revealed the two messages that the Italian government hoped to send to fairgoers and the world. The entrance was surmounted by a broad "wing," its tips stretching well beyond the building's vertical walls, resulting in the unmistakable imitation of an airplane. Partly an allusion to the planned transatlantic flight, the component was also a statement of Italy's commitment to aeronautics, itself a symbol of humanity's technological future. Above the wing rose an eighty-foot, prism glass tower suggesting the shape of the *Fascio Littorio*, the Italian Fascist Party emblem, to remind visitors of the political system that had guided the Kingdom of Italy in its role as a world-class technological leader.

Prince Ludovico Potenziani, an aristocrat with a proclivity for science, technology and economics—he was president of the International Institute of Agriculture—was appointed Italy's official commissioner for the fair, and the exhibition committee was chaired by the renowned inventor Guglielmo Marconi. The selection of such men, along with the pavilion's very shape, pointed openly to the style and manner in which Italy wanted to cast itself.

Potenziani arrived in Chicago on February 6, 1933, to oversee the pavilion's construction, which was managed by Chicagoan Alexander Capraro, the first Italian American in Illinois to be awarded an architect's license. The selected site was at the south end of the fair's Avenue of Flags, a broad promenade flanked by colorful, oversized banners reaching eighty feet above the pavement and inclined inward, leaving pedestrians with the impression that they were passing beneath a sprawling archway.

The admission gates to A Century of Progress World's Fair were unlocked with much fanfare on the morning of May 27, 1933, and within hours

Italian pavilion. *From* Official Book of the Flight of Gen. Italo Balbo *(1933).*

some 150,000 excited visitors were exploring the 427 acres of exhibits and attractions. The Italian pavilion, however, didn't officially open for another week. When, after a ribbon cutting ceremony, curious fairgoers were welcomed to enter, they found themselves in a vast reception hall bearing stylized murals and composite photographic panels of translucent glass, all rendering in heroic manner a sort of synopsis of what visitors would find in the building's 450 individual exhibits. So vast was the inventory of material on display, in fact, that the pavilion proved insufficient to house it all, and some exhibits spilled over into rented space in other buildings on the fairgrounds.

Although a requisite nod was made to Italy's natural beauty and its storied contributions to art and music, the true emphasis was squarely placed on technology and science. Pioneering technological accomplishments on the peninsula from Roman times forward—including architecture and construction materials and methods, engineering, roadbuilding and transportation—were detailed in individual displays in the pavilion's many rooms. The scientific brilliance of Galileo, Da Vinci, Malpighi, Galvani, Volta, Spallanzani and so many others was highlighted, along with their respective, world-changing work in physics, chemistry, biology, mathematics, astronomy and medicine. The new paths linking the continents—which had been opened by the dauntless explorers Marco Polo, Columbus, Verrazzano, Caboto and Vespucci—were recalled.

These historical themes were presented as a lead into the exhibition's core message, which was, of course, the great leaps of progress the country had made in the last decade under its Fascist regime. In transportation, Italy now boasted one of the world's largest airline networks, with an outstanding safety record. The national rail system had been increased by 30 percent, with telegraph and telephone service reporting similar expansion.

Thanks to its many mountain streams, Italy had been at the forefront in the development of clean hydroelectric generation, but with new and improved technology, the plants were churning out five times the electricity they were capable of producing in 1922.

Another momentous advance in transportation was the opening of the Milano-Varese Autostrada, which in 1924 became the world's first roadway dedicated exclusively for high-speed motorized traffic. Traveling up and down this and on streets and roads all over the country were the products of its much-respected automobile makers like FIAT, Alfa Romeo, Isotta Fraschini, Bianchi and Lancia, all recognized by motor enthusiasts around the globe as vehicles of high style and performance.

With three sides of their land surrounded by water, the Italians have always been a seafaring people, the pavilion's maritime section explained, and that tradition continued with its government-subsidized merchant marine fleet counted among the world's largest and most active. New, modern vessels were regularly launched from the busy shipbuilding yards in Genova and Naples to be put to work for Italian commerce or sold to foreign customers. Visitors could study scale models of the luxury liners *Rex* and *Conte di Savoia*, the pride of the Italian fleet. Only two months after the pavilion opened, the *Rex* would be awarded the Blue Riband upon completing a transatlantic voyage at a record-breaking average speed of 28.92 knots.

Americans, weathering the economic throes of the Great Depression, were particularly interested in the exhibits showcasing the Fascist government's ambitious civil engineering projects—the draining of the Pontine Marshes, the agricultural modernization initiatives and the expansion of national infrastructure—all of which tangibly improved the country while helping to relieve unemployment. During the weeks when the fair was just getting underway, newly elected president Franklin Delano Roosevelt had just created the Public Works Administration, a New Deal agency that would manage similar projects for the same purpose, though on a vastly greater scale. The earlier Italian successes provided a measure of encouragement and hope that the incipient American counterparts would have equally rewarding results.

The Italian pavilion offered more than stagnant exhibits and displays. Potenziani and his program administrators utilized the building as a venue for public lectures by a roster of distinguished international guests on a wide array of topics, ranging from the hard sciences to art and literature to political affairs. Newsreels, travelogues and other documentary films were regularly looped on an audio-visual hall screen, and with these features, the pavilion maintained its status as a popular stopping point.

A Century of Progress as a whole proved to be so wildly popular and such a boon for the local economy that its commissioners and the city council decided to extend it through the summer of the following year, a near-unprecedented run in the history of such events. A makeover was necessary to lure back at least some of the previous season's 1,139,000 attendees, so dozens of structures were demolished to make room for new attractions. The Italian pavilion, too, reopened for the 1934 season in modified form, substantially enlarged to accommodate those exhibits that had strayed elsewhere due to lack of space. The new additions also provided room for a ballroom and restaurant with indoor and al fresco seating. A bit more attention was given to art and Italian craftsmanship, with live Venetian glass blowing demonstrations presented in a modest, annexed building. But the pavilion's continuing purpose of casting Italy as a modern, cutting-edge nation was swiftly undermined by a new, wholly unrelated attraction at the fair.

This came about in the form of the Italian Village, the brainchild of Joseph Imburgio, a lawyer and the president of the Italo-American National Union, a local fraternal and mutual benefit society. The fair commission's original idea of a section of foreign "villages" was resurrected, finding a more positive reception than it had during its planning stage. Many foreign exhibitors had permanently withdrawn their exhibits at the end of the 1933 season, so something had to be offered to maintain the fair's international character. Situated near the lakefront, the various villages were built and maintained by the respective countries they were supposed to represent or privately owned creations by investors and entrepreneurs.

The concept of Italy entertained by Imburgio and his fellow American-born partners was the usual patchwork of demeaning stereotypes, Hollywood tropes and vague impressions gleaned from dinner table accounts of the "old country" by immigrant grandparents. If the rural hamlet from which an Italian American family traced its roots lacked indoor plumbing or electric lights in 1895, it was frequently interpreted to mean *all* of Italy lacked indoor plumbing and electric lights in 1933. Consequently, exhibits inside the Italian pavilion presented their ancestral homeland in so starkly unfamiliar a manner that they could scarcely relate to it.

The Italian Village, then, was intended to project a vision of Italy much more comfortably acceptable to second- or third-generation Italian Americans and the American public in general. Instead of a vibrant, industrialized nation claiming its place in the forefront of innovation and state-of-the-art technology, the village employed every stereotype to depict Italy as a sleepy, rural backwater populated by happily dancing peasants, singing waiters and lethargic donkeys. In fairness, parts of the concession were impressive, at least at first glance. Besides courtyards, piazzas and narrow cobblestone streets, the village's backdrop included scaled-down medieval towers and ancient Roman ruins. Americanized Italian fare could be enjoyed in the village's San Carlo restaurant, with the recent repeal of Prohibition allowing meals to be washed down with a glass of imported Chianti. In the end, though, the attraction's popularity couldn't produce a profit, and by late 1934 the Italian village corporation filed for bankruptcy with unpayable liabilities in excess of $100,000.

Potenziani and his staff, of course, didn't have to contend with this distraction of conflicting images when they were meticulously crafting their version of the nation's profile the previous year. But they were also faced with other concerns that went beyond the pavilion and its exhibits. As summer approached, letters warning of violent acts being planned against Italo Balbo began showing up in the office mailbox of Chicago's Italian consulate. As in 1929, radicals, both Italian and American, objected to his despised presence in the country, and their newspapers and pamphlets were calling for organized protests. The letters received by Consul General Giuseppe Castruccio, however, threatened bomb blasts. Although he dismissed them as most likely the work of harmless cranks, Castruccio nonetheless shared them with the fair authorities and the Chicago police, prompting enhanced security measures to be taken around the Italian pavilion and all of the other venues at which Balbo and his airmen were scheduled to be received.

Their planes would be anchored at Navy Pier, under around-the-clock guard, for the duration of the visit, and spectators were allowed to view them at close distance from the pier's north promenade. *Regia Aeronautica* major Carlo Tempesti, in charge of the flight's logistical preparations in Chicago, therefore requested increased surveillance at the squadron's mooring area.

PREPARATION FOR THE DECENNALE CRUISE

P reparation for the Decennale cruise, by necessity much more intense than all the previous mass flights combined, was set in motion. The official name of this aerial expedition was *Croceira Aerea del Decennale*, or Tenth Anniversary Aerial Cruise, to mark the decade that had passed since the Fascist Party's march on Rome, but this was inaccurate, since that event took place in 1922. And while Mussolini was named prime minister that year, other political parties still played a role in running the country, with cabinet and administrative positions and through elected representatives in the Italian Parliament. It wasn't until 1925, when Mussolini assumed dictatorial powers, that the regime held complete and exclusive control of the Italian government. The more logical and occasionally cited commemoration was the tenth anniversary of the *Regia Aeronautica*, an event that took place one exact decade before the cruise. In either case, the theme played heavily on Italian Fascism and the spirit of youthful energy and progress that it purported to represent.

The aircraft selected for the enterprise was the latest version of the well-proven S-55, now designated the SM-55X, much improved over the earlier models used by De Pinedo in his 1927 American tour and in the subsequent mass flights across the Mediterranean and South Atlantic.

The builder of this remarkable aircraft was *Societa Idrovolanti di Alta Italia* (SIAI). The Upper Italy Hydroplane Company was founded in 1915, the year Italy entered World War I. Based in the town of Sesto Calende along the Lago Maggiore shoreline, the company focused exclusively on seaplanes, which, particularly after the Armistice, were believed by many both in and outside of Italy to be the type of aircraft destined to shape aviation's future.

With the nation's 4,700 miles of coastline, Italians naturally gravitated toward planes that used water as runways. But on a broader scale, hydroplane proponents like De Pinedo argued that most great cities around the world had risen on or near a body of water—whether ocean, lake, sea or river—and therefore were immediately reachable without constructing costly inland airports. Among the most fervent seaplane enthusiasts, De Pinedo even envisioned their eventual use by everyday people who could commute to work from suburban ponds to municipal parking ports.

The seaplanes and flying boats built by SIAI first gained international attention when the Schneider Trophy races, canceled during the war years, were resumed in 1919. The company supplied the Italian team's entry for that year, an S-13 biplane flying boat piloted by wartime ace Guido Janello. Held in Bournemouth in the English Channel, the event was plagued by so perilously thick a fog that all of the competing planes dropped out except the persistent S-16, which completed the entire course. Though deprived a victory by default, as the judges ruled that Janello had briefly flown outside a course marker while whipping his way around the mist-covered bay at about 120 miles per hour, the event allowed SIAI to showcase the performance capabilities of its products to the world.

The following year, the firm hired thirty-eight-year-old Alessandro Marchetti, a well-seasoned aircraft designer who had built his first plane back in 1909. Gifted with an innovative mind that combined mechanical ingenuity with eye-catching aesthetics, he soon rose to the position of technical director and chief design engineer. His ideas so dominated the company's product line that his surname was eventually incorporated into the SIAI brand, known thereafter as Savoia-Marchetti (since the company's founding, its planes bore the brand name of Savoia, in honor of the Kingdom of Italy's ruling dynasty). The model number designation prefix was likewise eventually changed from "S" to "SM."

Marchetti began experimenting with the S-55 flying boat as early as 1923, intending to develop it as a torpedo bomber for the newly created *Regia Aeronautica*. His blueprints revealed a design radically different from anything built to that date. The plane looked like a sort of flying catamaran, composed of

Vintage SIAI advertisement. *From Pagine di Storia (1982).*

two separate spruce and ash hulls connected by a broad wing just under eighty feet in length. Lightweight but highly durable aluminum tubes extended from the hulls to support two pairs of rudders and tail fins. Along with housing fuel tanks, each hull featured front and rear machine gun stations. The plane's torpedo load was carried beneath the center of the sturdy, massive wing. The cockpit was situated in the center of the wing with the power plant, placed on pylons high above it to minimize contact with water spray. The power plant itself consisted of two, tandem-mounted, back-to-back engines, each turning a two-blade, contra-rotating air screw in pusher-puller arrangement.

Marchetti also introduced a commercial variant of the aircraft in which the hulls were converted to passenger and cargo space. Recognizing that he'd come up with a winner, he continued improving the plane's design to increase its utility and performance. His diligence brought quick dividends, with the S-55 setting fourteen world records for distance, speed, altitude and load in 1926 alone. As aerodynamically refined as it was quite seaworthy, the streamlined, twin-hulled flying boat would stand as one of Alessandro Marchetti's masterpiece creations.

By the time the active planning of the 1933 mass flight was underway, the latest model of the plane, the SM-55X had gone into production.

SM-55X. *Italian Air Force Historical Office.*

52

Isotta Fraschini engine. *From Official Book of the Flight of Gen. Italo Balbo (1933).*

The most significant alteration was the upgraded power plant, now consisting of two 750-horsepower, Isotta Fraschini eighteen-cylinder engines, each driving three-blade variable pitch airscrews to produce a top speed of 174 miles per hour and a 16,440-foot maximum ceiling.

The cockpit was fitted with a state-of-the-art instrument cluster, and plane-to-plane and air-to-surface communication was maintained through a four-hundred-watt short- and long-wave radio transmitter, capable of sending messages as far as one thousand miles. The instrument cluster featured a radio compass to indicate the direction from which incoming messages were sent, a valuable navigational tool for taking bearings. Two antennae were fastened at the front and rear of the aircraft, and the radio equipment was powered by a wind-driven exterior generator. Taillights on the rudders helped make the SM-55X visible at night or in foggy conditions. Literally nothing was overlooked, and Marchetti assured Balbo that the flying boat would "perform like an Olympic champion."

As with the South Atlantic cruise, each of the participating aircraft would be manned by a commander (lead pilot), a copilot/navigator, a noncom radio operator and a mechanic. Selection of the applicants was based on their records and exam scores. Those chosen were awarded with the elite distinction of being an *"Atlantico."* Per Balbo's policy, and with the exception of a group of senior officers, none of the pilots selected for participation had any seaplane or mass flight experience. Their training was formally initiated at the newly created *Scuola della Navigazione Aerea di Alto Mare* (School for High Seas Aerial Navigation) on May 2, 1931, where they were sequestered for two years, although they were granted weekend free time twice a month.

The rigorous curriculum incorporated courses on practical and theoretical mathematics, physics, aerodynamics, thermodynamics, navigation and radio technology. The mechanics, all of them sergeants or corporals, were sent off to the factories of SIAI and Isotta Fraschini to immerse themselves in the details of the plane, the power plant and every other component, as well as troubleshooting and repair techniques. Every man was further required to take English classes so, at the very minimum, they could manage basic communication in that language.

Cockpit. *From* My Air Armada *(1934)*.

Top physical condition was maintained through the regimen of daily calisthenics and a carefully planned diet. Field training had the aviators boarding small gunboats on exceptionally rough seas to experience and acclimate themselves to the rolling and tossing of ocean waves. To complete their competency, the pilots had to train for and demonstrate proficiency in takeoff, flying and landing in every type of weather, both at night and day, with varying loads and with and without instrumentation. Exercises under these conditions were performed both individually and in groups to ensure tight maneuverability in relation to the mass flight pattern.

For his second in command, Balbo would have undoubtedly selected Umberto Maddalena, architect of the South Atlantic flight, had he not been tragically killed when his plane exploded midflight in March 1931. Instead, the position went to General Aldo Pellegrini, the director of the training school, who, at forty-five, was the flight's oldest participant. His military service uninterrupted since the 1911 Italo-Turkish War, Pellegrini originally served in the Royal Italian Navy and was assigned to its burgeoning air division in 1915. Like De Pinedo and so many others, he transferred to the *Regia Aeronautica*. Calm, methodical and with a steady demeanor, he quickly distinguished himself not only as a first-tier pilot but also as a skilled administrator. Pellegrini closely assisted in the preparation

General Aldo Pellegrini. *From Official Book of the Flight of Gen. Italo Balbo (1933).*

of the Mediterranean cruises and the mass flight to Brazil and was universally recognized as Balbo's right-hand man in the execution of the Decennale air cruise.

Next to Pellegrino was Lieutenant Colonel Stefano Cagna, who had served as Balbo's personal instructor when he obtained his pilot license back in 1926, as well as copilot for the South Atlantic voyage. A participant in the successful dropping of survival supplies to the Italia airship crew trapped on the desolate Arctic wastes in 1928, he had also worked on the feasibility and planning commissions for the mass flight programs.

Lieutenant Colonel Ulisse Longo, assistant director of the Orbatello training school, joined Pellegrini and Cagna as lead commandants and Balbo's consultants and advisors of the upcoming cruise. The entire roster of participants, including Balbo and his staff, consisted of fifty-four commissioned officers and forty-nine noncoms. That number would occasionally be exceeded, as the planes were sometimes scheduled to pick up or drop off ground support staff, visiting officials and journalists along the way.

Other senior officers headed special commissions to handle the various components of the flight's broader infrastructure, such as fuel and supply procurement, establishment and staffing of layover stations, meteorological services and communication systems—all under a central coordinating office.

The ground support apparatus, which would prove to be the most impressive component of the enterprise, was complex and thorough. According to the finalized route plan, designed for the most efficient use of fuel and the range capabilities of S55-X, the outbound route would have six layover points and surface support stations at Amsterdam, Londonderry, Reykjavik, Cartwright (Labrador), Shediac (New Brunswick) and Montreal. A seventh base was placed in Julianehaab (since renamed Qaqortoq) on the southern tip of Greenland, but only for weather monitoring. Among those manning that station, incidentally, was a German geophysicist recommended by Balbo's friend Wolfgang Von Gronau.

After Chicago, the return trip would encompass a visit to New York City, with the eastbound Atlantic crossing being launched from Shoal Harbor (Newfoundland). From there the squadron would either fly to Ireland again or southward to the Azores, depending on the meteorological forecasts.

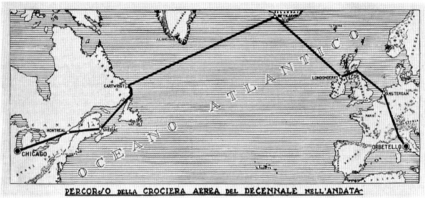

PERCORSO DELLA CROCIERA AEREA DEL DECENNALE NELL'ANDATA

Top: Decennale crew members. *Italian Air Force Historical Office.*

Bottom: Decennale route. *From* Official Book of the Flight of Gen. Italo Balbo *(1933).*

Between the layover points, eleven ships and submarines shared multiple duties of shuttling supplies to the bases, patrolling the route and maintaining surface support through radio communications with the planes. Once the actual North Atlantic crossing began, the four vessels provided by the Royal Italian Navy, the submarines *Balilla* and *Millelire* and the trawlers *Matteucci* and *Biglieri*, would position themselves beneath the flight path in respective patrol zones about 250 miles apart. Several English and Danish whaling boats were borrowed or placed on standby between Ireland and Iceland, all with Italian officers on board. Canadian ice breakers were hired to clear the frozen passages, inlets and bays around the bases at Labrador and Newfoundland.

The workhorse of the fleet would again be the reliable, swift-moving yacht *Alice*, which carried a rescue plane on board and was equipped with a weather balloon. Ships, land bases and the flying boats were all integrated into a complex radio network, transmitting regular reports on air temperature, water temperature, wind speed and direction, barometric pressure and forecasts.

Radio communications had proven sporadic and faulty during the South Atlantic cruise, and improving that critical component was a priority. Organization of the surface-to-air communication network, the most extensive and complex assembled to that date, was placed in the capable hands of Lieutenant Colonel Mario Infante. The task started by identifying and assessing the existing wire, cable and radio facilities along the proposed flight path and working out ways to equip the stretches where none existed. The goal was to ensure an unbroken chain of communication along every inch of the six-thousand-mile path from the Italian ministry in Rome to the North American bases. Whether land based, in the air or on the water, each station in the network kept a log of transmission that was broadcast, either directly or relayed. Weather bulletins would be transmitted every hour to the planes when in flight and twice a day between bases for the quiet spells during layovers.

Infante secured allocated frequencies from the international radio communication authorities, an absolute necessity to keep the lines clear, and these were shared with the coast guards and navies of nations bordering the ocean route, which were invited to monitor the flight's progress.

Foreign participation was further integrated into the system with an offer of assistance from Hernand Behn, president of the International Telephone and Telegraph Corporation, who reached out to the Italian Air Ministry as soon as plans for the transatlantic crossing were announced. Shortly thereafter, Infante and Pellegrini traveled to New York to consult with the company's engineers. Other American and Canadian communication entities, public or privately owned, wishing to play a role in the development of what was clearly a historical milestone, followed ITT's lead in volunteering their expertise and resources.

Eventually, the partnership grew to include the U.S. Army, Navy and Coast Guard Communications Offices, the U.S. and Canadian National Weather

SM-55X radio instruments. *From* Cieli E Mari *(1973).*

Services, the Marconi Wireless Company of Canada and the Canadian Pacific Railroad Company. All of these partners generously placed their transmission and weather monitoring facilities at Infante's disposal. Shared technical information allowed for remedial measures to be worked out in advance, particularly overcoming transmission difficulties rendered by

Lieutenant Colonel Mario Infante and U.S. Naval Reserve lieutenant commander Ellery W. Stone work out transatlantic radio communications network details at an International Telephone & Telegraph facility. *Communications for Italian Transatlantic Flight, Proceedings, August 1934, U.S. Naval Institute.*

frequent magnetic or electrical storms along the route. The network was fixed in place by spring, undergoing multiple tests runs in which messages on the dedicated frequencies were seamlessly and clearly received to and from Orbatello and North America, as well as the support vessels and stopping points in between. It was, according to a report published in an American electronic communications journal, "the most ambitious chain of radio, cable, and wire communications ever attempted for an aerial venture, in fact, for any world event."

Each layover point was under the command of a senior officer, typically a lieutenant colonel or a major, who in some instances also served as a special liaison to the local government of the host country, selecting a base site and securing permission for its installation. The operational center was typically a rented building near the landing point and was staffed by a meteorologist, a radio/telegraph operator, a cartographer, a quartermaster, a team of mechanics and similar specialists. Substitute crewmen were also on hand in case any active members fell ill or otherwise became incapacitated while the flight was in progress. The base commanders made room and board arrangements for the surface support staff members and flight crews and managed the procurement of spare parts, provisions and fuel supplies. He was also responsible for laying out the landing and mooring points to safely accommodate and refuel the two dozen large flying boats. Cartwright, a remote outpost on the desolate coast of Newfoundland, with no available lodging and minimal infrastructure, was the exception. There the multi-tasking *Alice* would dock to act as the base and serve as an ad hoc hotel for Balbo and his men.

The structural composition of the air fleet consisted of two units, or "storms," with each storm composed of two groups. Each group was divided into two squads of three aircraft. The four groups were identifiable by black, red, white or green markings on their rudders, with stars for the leading half of the companies and discs for the rest. The planes themselves were individually distinguishable by the first four letters of the name of their respective commanders boldly painted across the underside of the wings. Preceded by the letter *I*, Italy's international radio prefix, the markings served as each plane's radio call letters.

Every aircraft was equipped with a life raft, and impermeable flight suits were worn by the crews in the event of a crash and submersion in the water. Along with their personal toiletries, the aviators hung their service uniforms in one of the hulls, into which they were to change before appearing in public. Their full dress uniforms were sent in advance to Montreal, the final stopping point before Chicago. Coffee, water and fruit were the staple rations, and as an unexpected gift, the Italian Agricultural Society furnished each plane with a crate of freshly picked peaches just prior to departure.

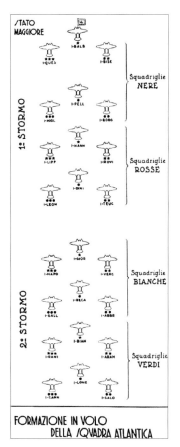

Decennale order of formation. *From* Official Book of the Flight of Gen. Italo Balbo *(1933).*

Once in the air, the planes would maintain strict formation but fly at slightly staggered altitudes, each positioned a few feet lower than the one in front of it so the entire squadron was visible to every pilot. Upon approaching a landing point, the storms would group into a V formation, with Balbo's plane in the lead, and glide down to the water surface three at a time.

Leading the first three planes of the Black Group was the I-BALB, the squadron's flagship, with Balbo as lead pilot and Cagna as copilot. Joining the rest of the crew was technical expert Major Carlo Pezzani of the Aeronautical Engineering Corps, on board to advise on procedures to be taken should any serious mechanical or structural problems arise while in the air.

Behind Balbo's plane were I-BISE (Captain Attilio Biseo) and I-QUES (Captain Luigi Questa). The second division of the Black Group was led by I-PELL (General Pellegrini, Balbo's right-hand man during the enterprise) and then I-MIGL (Captain Alessandro Miglia) and I-BORG (Captain Bruno Borghetti).

Heading the Red Group was I-NANN (Captain Umberto Nannini), followed by I-L-LIPP (Captain Antonio Lippi), I-ROVI (Captain Umberto Rovis), I-DINI (Captain Mario Baldini), I-LEON (Captain Leonello Leone) and I-TEUCI (Captain Giuseppe Teucci).

Next was the White Group, led by I-GIOR (Captain Gennaro Giordano), along with I-NAPO (Captain Silvio Napoli), I-VERC (Captain Alessandro Vercelloni), I-RECA (Captain Enea Recagno), I-GALL (Captain Luigi Gallo) and I-ABBR (Captain Renato Abbriata).

The two squads of the Green Group were led by I-BIAN (Captain Vincenzo Biani), I-RANI (Captain Celso Ranieri) and I-ARAM (Captain Mario Aramu). At the rear of the formation was Lieutenant Colonel Longo in I-LONG, I-CANN (Captain Letterio Cannistracci) and I-CALO (Captain Jacopo Caló). Joining this group was a reserve SM-55X, piloted by Captain Stefano Trimboli with a full crew.

Orbatello SM-55X staging area. *From* Cieli E Mari *(1973).*

Everything was firmly in place by the beginning of June 1933. Two weeks before the Decennelle cruise was launched, Balbo held a press conference:

> *Shortly, we shall attempt to fly to America with a squadron of 24 large aircraft. I believe that in a technical sense, we have sufficiently covered every conceivable detail in organizing an enterprise of this scale. I would go so far as to say that the most difficult tasks are already behind us. In view of these logistical preparations, we are confident that the odds of our success are favorable.*
>
> *But please note that I said we shall "attempt" to fly to America. In the event of exceptionally adverse weather or any other situation that might impose needless risk, I intend to order the squadron to return to Italy.*

Clearly, the bold, even reckless derring-do that popular imagination had long associated with flying had no place in this enterprise. But Balbo's statement, and the support apparatus he had created, was an indicator that aviation was maturing. Setting new records and attaining aeronautical milestones were still necessary and important, of course, but the point had been reached where the application of the best available technology and scrupulous planning were the saner, more practical way to proceed.

EXECUTION OF THE DECENNALE CRUISE

Reveille sounded at 4:00 a.m. on July 1, 1933. No breakfast was served. Coffee and fruit would be available on the planes once they were in the air. Instead, everyone stood at attention in the base's courtyard for an earlier than normal flag raising ceremony, the still unrisen sun's pink and purple glows just starting to tint the eastern sky. Only the bugle's call to the colors and the distant squawk of seagulls broke the stillness of the morning as all eyes fixed on the Royal Tricolor as it reached the top of the mast. A moment of continued silence, and then came Balbo's order to hoist anchors. "Long Live the King!" the aviators answered in unison before dispersing to man their flying boats.

During the week prior to takeoff, the families of all of the flight's participants were invited to visit Orbatello to spend casual time with their departing sons or husbands. Balbo's wife, Emanuella, arrived with photographs of their two daughters and son, which the air minister proudly posted in his cockpit. The traditional blessing of the planes and personnel, during which a Catholic priest entrusted them to the care of *La Madonna Di Loreto* (Our Lady of Loreto), the patroness of aviators, had also been performed days earlier. So, with the exception of some curious fishermen who paused their morning work to watch from their distant boats, no one but the Orbatello ground crew was present to witness the departure.

By 5:30 a.m., the planes were boarded, and the silence of that early summer morning was shattered by a chorus of the monstrous growls of their mighty Isotta Fraschini engines. With I-BALB in the lead, the groups

Left: Transfer to water surface. *From* Cieli E Mari *(1973)*.

Below: Air fleet flagship. *From* My Air Armada *(1934)*.

Opposite: Flight in process. *Italian Air Force Historical Office.*

lifted off the blue waters of the Tyrrhenian Sea in an ordered sequence. They circled overhead until joined by the final triad and reserve machine. Then, like a graceful flock of migrating geese, they assumed formation and flew into the brightening northeastern sky.

In about two hours, they were approaching the Alps, and the squadron gradually pulled itself up to an altitude of thirteen thousand feet as it crossed the rugged, snow-covered peaks. For some undisclosed reason, the Swiss government had imposed restrictions on air space over the St. Gotthard Pass, a region that happened to lie directly beneath the originally planned route. This was a relatively minor inconvenience, but the resulting detour meant an increase in fuel consumption and an encounter with rougher weather than the sunny and tranquil conditions reported over St. Gotthard.

Upon clearing the Swiss border, the squadron followed the course of the Rhine, straddling the French and German lands that were separated by the winding river. Although buffeting winds persisted, cloud cover occasionally broke, and the planes dropped altitude to the point where the seemingly unending series of farms, factories, hamlets and cities were distinguishable in sharp detail. Finally, after shifting away from the river, they reached Amsterdam at 11:30 a.m.

Descending to 750 feet, the *Atlantici* could clearly see that its streets were filled with spectators, all anxious to welcome them. The landing point was on the city's busy main canal, on which its usual, intense activity had been temporarily suspended to provide a safe, unobstructed descent zone. The canals of Amsterdam are numerous, well over one hundred, but relatively shallow at a typical depth of six to twelve feet. While sufficient for the tugboats and barges that made up most of their traffic, this water level imposes a challenge for seaplanes, alighting at high speed. Pilots must tap into their most well-honed skills to maintain their machines in an uncompromisingly straight and level position when touching down on the surface. Too steep an angle or contact with floating or unseen debris during this critical maneuver could result in trouble.

The intense field training undergone by the *Atlantici*, of course, included handling this and every other imaginable situation, but this did not prevent

Wreck of the I-DINI. *From* My Air Armada *(1934)*.

tragedy on the squadron's very first day out. The I-DINI, the lead aircraft of the second "red" company, suddenly did a full flip, nose first, on contact with the water. Lead pilot Mario Baldini, copilot Lieutenant Amelio Novelli and radio operator Sergeant Demetrio Jaria were able to extract themselves from the wreckage, but Sergeant Ugo Quintavalle, the crew's mechanic, did not emerge from the water alive.

The tragic incident naturally cast an impenetrable pall over what should have been a joyous occasion. All the welcoming celebrations planned for the Italians by their Dutch hosts were abruptly canceled. The survivors of the crash were taken to a hospital and treated for their injuries, while Quintavalle's remains went to the morgue to be prepared for transfer back to Orbatello for burial with full military honors.

Balbo and the other pilots, emotionally shaken, sequestered themselves in their accommodations at the city's Amstel Hotel to mourn their lost comrade and speculate what caused the plane to flip. After inspection of the wreckage and crash site, and the surviving crew members' account of the incident, the most probable explanation was that Baldini, despite his years of experience piloting flying boats reaching back to the world war, made a miscalculation regarding his plane's angle of contact with the water, causing one of the hulls to scrape the bottom of the shallow canal. The high speed of travel when sudden, hard contact was made caused the plane to literally somersault nose first and rest in the water on its back. Quintavalle was killed on impact.

The mechanics spent the rest of the day fueling and meticulously reinspecting their own planes, now moored in the canal, before the predawn departure. In lieu of the canceled festivities, Balbo received guests and well-wishers in the quiet privacy of his hotel room. Among those who called was the famous British journalist Lady Grace Margaret Drummond-Hay, distinguished by her travels around the world to cover aviation-related stories, and Balbo's friend and colleague Wolfgang Von Gronau, who had just landed in Amsterdam to personally wish him good fortune. The Dutch aircraft designer Anton Fokker, whose planes played such a major role during the Great War, also stopped in to meet the Italian air minister and extend his best wishes. That evening, these and other visitors joined Balbo and his officers for a modest dinner held in place of the congratulatory reception and banquet that was originally scheduled.

Funeral of Sergeant Quintavalle. *Italian Air Force Historical Office.*

With the reserve plane filling the position of Baldini's irreparable aircraft, the entire squadron managed a trouble-free departure at 6:00 a.m., witnessed by thousands of the city's residents who, despite the early hour, crowded the banks and bridges around the canal to see the Italians off on their seven-hundred-mile journey to Northern Ireland. The aviators encountered fluctuating weather conditions while crossing the North Sea and then the English coast, varying from rain and heavy cloud cover to sudden bursts of sunshine, but there were no surprises, as the squadron's radio operators were receiving continual updates from service radio stations. Scotland was reached by 10:00 a.m., which, Balbo reported, brought to mind the gracefully plaintive melodies of *Lucia Di Lammermoor*, Gaetano Donizetti's Bel Canto opera that was set in the misty, seventeenth-century Scottish moors.

One hour later, they were approaching Londonderry. The planes dropped altitude and traced two great circles over the north Irish city under a brilliant, sunny sky. As in Amsterdam, the aviators could see that thousands of its citizens were in the streets in anticipation of their arrival. Anchorage was set up at the point where the River Foyle flows into the vast Lough Foyle Bay before emptying into the Atlantic Ocean, and every pilot executed a smooth landing. A British squadron appeared overhead, with its planes tipping their wings to salute the Italians.

Once on shore, Balbo was greeted by British Air Marshal Sir Robert Clark-Hall, Industrial Minister of Northern Ireland Sir John Milne Barbour and layover point commander Captain Gino Bertoli. A contingent of British soldiers presented arms, after which the *Atlantici* were taken to Guildhall, the stately Londonderry City Council building, which with its soaring clocktower, stained-glass windows and gargantuan 3,132-pipe organ bore all the appearance of a great cathedral. There, Lord Mayor Dudley McCorkell, adorned in official mayoral robes, presided over the official welcome in the presence of what appeared to be every habitant of the town waving miniature Italian and British flags.

Bertoli had arranged for the aviators to stay at Troy Hall, a turreted, lavishly furnished Victorian manor a short walk away. Once settled in, Balbo and his chief officers examined weather reports wired in from the Iceland and Greenland bases, none of which was promising. With that, Balbo made the decision to wait in Ireland until less threatening conditions developed. No doubt the fatal accident in Amsterdam weighed heavily on his decision for an extended layover. As he put it, they were not participating in a speed contest.

In recruiting candidates for the Decennale cruise, the Air Ministry had emphasized the chance to visit foreign lands, so Balbo encouraged his men to explore the city to pass time during the layover. The noncoms and junior officers, typically single and in their early twenties, had no trouble finding young Irish ladies who were quite agreeable to showing them around town. Meanwhile, Balbo and a handful of officers hired a car to take them to the boundary line separating Northern Ireland and the Irish Free State, just west of Londonderry. The border guards allowed the Italians to cross over at the toll cost of Balbo's autograph. Not more than a few minutes were spent on the soil of what would later become the Republic of Ireland, but word of the occasion raced rapidly. The next day, Balbo received a lighthearted telegram from Irish Free State president Eamon de Valera, expressing his delight with the air minister's visit to his country, however brief.

Reports of a stalled system of hash weather over the next leg of the cruise delayed its resumption for yet another day. Balbo, Pellegrini and Cagna spent the time by honoring an invitation to the summer manor of the British air minister and Marquess of Londonderry Lord Charles Stewart, an ancient country estate near Belfast. British planes were provided to transport the Italians, British Air Marshal Clark-Hall and several other officials on the ninety-four-mile trip, and upon takeoff, Balbo was shocked to see the pilot and crew light up cigarettes. Smoking was absolutely forbidden on the Italian planes, and although he himself was a smoker when not in the air, he couldn't bring himself to accept a cigarette offered by one of the Britons.

Balbo and Lord Stewart were already acquainted, having met at several international conferences, and greeted each other as old friends. Since neither was fluent in the other's language, conversation was carried in French. With typical, self-deprecatory humor, Balbo later recalled that the British nobleman spoke flawlessly while he stumbled his way through in "an infamous Italian parody of Parisian pronunciation."

Back in the Londonderry hotel that evening, reports arrived confirming that weather over the route to Iceland was improving and that a prompt resumption of the journey should be made before adverse conditions returned. The planes were refueled and checked daily, so there was nothing to delay takeoff the following morning. The squadron circled the city several times as a farewell gesture, to the sound of church bells, sirens and horn blasts from every boat in the harbor returning the salute.

Despite the initial indications of favorable weather, conditions fluctuated dramatically as the Italians made their way toward Iceland. Balbo had to repeatedly instruct his pilots to adjust speed, altitude and formation as they

Balbo and the Marquis of Londonderry. *From* My Air Armada *(1934).*

maneuvered for hours through thick fogs, torrents of rain, buffeting lateral or counterwinds and driving snow, all in random succession.

The planes were still being mercilessly pelted with blinding rain drops when, with 955 miles and six and a half hours of rough flying behind them, they reached Reykjavik. Both landing and mooring were difficult under the stormy conditions, requiring a full hour to secure all the aircraft to their buoys. The rain eventually abated, but the temperature was turning frigid as Balbo and the aviators were ferried to shore by a fleet of motorboats. This had been foreseen by the Decennale's planning commissions, of course, and each crew member had been furnished with a fur-lined leather coat and hat that, one of the pilots later quipped, made them look like genuine Nordics.

The weather, they immediately discovered, had not deterred thousands of Icelanders, who turned out in the streets to greet them. The first to greet Balbo was the little daughter of Prime Minister Ásgeir Ásgeirsson, who welcomed him with an armful of flowers. All of the principal civil and military authorities followed, extending their own gestures of welcome, after which a line of cars whisked the Italians to their place of lodging.

Captain Antonio Altomare, chief of the Reykjavik base, had reserved rooms for the Atlantici at Hotel Borg. Barely three years old, with stylish Art Deco furnishings, it was the city's pride and the accommodation of choice for visiting foreign celebrities and diplomats. After a modest supper, the pilots busied themselves completing their required daily reports, and Balbo, Pellegrini and the other chief officers reviewed the squadron's performance and the upcoming challenge of the journey's next leg, the perilous flight to North America.

It was only when they prepared for bed that the Italians remembered that the skies never completely darken even in the dead of night during Icelandic summers. When the thin, blue curtains in their rooms failed to prevent glimmers of daylight striking their pillows, some solved the problem by hanging the bedspreads over the windows. The following morning, it became evident that the layover would be considerably prolonged, as reports from the Greenland base and the support ships warned of persisting dangers.

Little had been prepared in the way of festivities, and certainly nothing remotely close to what was awaiting the squadron in the United States. The only affair of note was a formal dinner held at the prime minister's

Arrival in Iceland. *From* My Air Armada *(1934).*

home, where dinner conversations were hampered by a limited supply of translators. The difficulties persisted until one of the guests hit on the idea of speaking in Latin. Balbo, having a passable knowledge of the ancient tongue of his Italic ancestors, was delighted, and everyone was amused as the mode of communication switched, if somewhat falteringly, to that language.

Any further celebrations during the layover occurred not on land but aboard several ocean liners that happened to dock at Reykjavik concurrent with the squadron's arrival. Each of their respective captains—German, English, Swedish and Danish—invited the *Atlantici* to enjoy recreational activities and evenings of dining and dancing on their vessels, offers that were gratefully accepted. Journalists from both America and Europe were among the passengers of the ships, having made the journey in specific hope of encountering Balbo, and he was endlessly beset with requests for an interview. He and those of his companions who did speak with newsmen from the United States were forewarned that the massive welcome awaiting them in Chicago would far exceed their most imaginative expectations.

Hundreds of tourists from the liners stopped by the Borg Hotel, seeking autographs and an opportunity to meet the aviators. The airmen, reticent and not quite prepared for their sudden celebrity status, politely accepted invitations to lunch or dinner at a local restaurant or simply a stroll through town. Off they went with their new friends, individually or in small groups, but always maintaining a cheerful but proper and courteous military deportment. Everyone still had his daily duties, the junior officers and mechanics tending to the planes and the officers joining briefings on the flight schedule, but the many hours of pleasant socialization with Icelanders and tourists of a dozen different nationalities made the layover anything but boring.

Some of the airmen joined in daytrips to view the island's famous geysers, while others tried their hand at salmon fishing as the layover dragged on. Balbo, meanwhile, was surprised to find another old acquaintance. The accomplished Danish explorer Knud Rasmussen had just arrived in town, and along with Pellegrini and Longo, they spent an entire day together. Famous for his many milestone Arctic expeditions, Rasmussen had met the Italian air minister during a visit to Italy and generously shared an abundance of geophysical details on the frigid zones over which the squadron would shortly traverse. Although the Greenland base, serving only as a weather station, was not set up as a landing point, there was a possibility that emergency circumstances might force the squadron to use it as such. Rasmussen, intimately familiar with the giant, ice-covered land mass and the inlets and bays of its jagged coast, advised the Italians of his best options for a safe landing point. This information was gratefully shared with the lead pilots during the next of their daily meetings at the hotel.

On Sunday, July 9, all of the Italians went to morning Mass at Christ the King Cathedral, at the time the only Catholic church on the entire, overwhelmingly Lutheran island. Their attendance was motivated by the comforting familiarity of the sacred rite as much as religious piety, and they embraced this solitary reminder of home in such an otherwise thoroughly foreign place. In fact, at one point it occurred to Balbo that fresh fruit, so abundant in Italy, must certainly be a rarer treat for Icelanders and that the crates of peaches stocked on his planes would make a suitable gift to reciprocate their hospitality. That pleasant plan dissolved when he learned from the pilots that nearly all of the peaches had already been consumed by the crewmen.

Finally, the much-anticipated forecasts of a favorable turn in the weather began arriving, and the departure date was set for Tuesday, July 11. The long days of idly passing time were over as the entire Decennale apparatus snapped back into action. At 1,500 miles, the next leg of the cruise would be the longest, most isolated and most dangerous stretch of the cruise. The fleet would be blazing a path over the most frigid zone of North Atlantic yet to be opened by any aviator. Its fuel tanks topped to the capacity necessary to complete the trip, each plane would face the daunting task, further burdened by the additional weight of fuel needed to complete the frigid, 1,500-mile trek. Only during the test runs at Orbatello had the SM-55Xs borne such a load.

The captains of the support ships were instructed to position their vessels in zones assigned to them, and the ground staffs at Julianenhaab and Cartwright were put on alert. But when the moment of takeoff arrived, I-BALB, the squadron's leader, could not pull itself above the water. A second attempt was made, with the plane speeding across the surface, its grinding engines pushed to the redline, but again no lift. Mystified, Balbo ordered everyone back to the moorings and held an impromptu conference with Pellegrini and the other lead pilots, all in the presence of the hundreds of Icelanders assembled to see them off.

Captain Questa was the next to try getting his own plane airborne, but his attempts were equally fruitless. The impromptu conference determined the culprit to be the seemingly light breezes blowing in from the land, which, under normal circumstances, would present no obstacle. But their strength, while modest, conspiring with the burden of the extra fuel load, was just formidable enough to hinder a trouble-free lift. The suggestion was made to move the takeoff stretch to another section of the island and away from the wind, but that process would take time, and as it was already late morning, Balbo decided to postpone departure for one more day.

The troublesome winds persisted the following morning, but now the aviators were prepared to overcome the problem by veering leeward as they moved across the water while accelerating to liftoff speed. In just over a minute, the hulls of Balbo's aircraft rose from the surface, rapidly soaring upward like an uncaged canary. One by one, the rest of the planes followed and, assuming formation, vanished from sight by 7:30 a.m.

An hour in, the squadron found itself enveloped by fog from which no shift in altitude provided an escape. Balbo ordered an extended formation, a standard precaution that increases the planes' distances from one another and further staggers their altitudes to lessen the chance of a collision during times of poor visibility. For the rest of the morning, the aviators saw nothing but dull and thick gray mist undulating in every direction. Even their own wingtips were not discernable. Relief was found from the brain-numbing monotony only by the surface temperature, wind speed and barometric pressure readings regularly transmitted from the support ships and Julianenhaab. Balbo roll called the crews in between the weather reports for confirmation that everyone was well and keeping pace.

After a while, gray darkened to black as the planes burst into the teeth of an even more blinding storm. The planes pitched and bounced, but escaping the turbulence was risky. The air temperature was already only a few degrees above freezing, and an ascent to colder elevations above the fog and rain would inevitably result in ice formation on the aircraft wings and, as a result, certain catastrophe. After discussing the situation with Pezzani, Cagna and Pellegrini, Balbo decided to take a calculated chance and ordered the squadron to climb above the storm.

Visibility improved upon surmounting the rain clouds, but the air temperature dropped dangerously low as predicted. The extended formation order was reversed, and the flying boats were instructed to close ranks to about three hundred feet from one another. The expectation was that the concentration of heat generated by forty-eight engines and the exhaust gases they released into the air would combine to form a sort of bubble of warmth around the planes and therefore avoid the dreaded ice formation.

Thankfully, the storm beneath them passed, and the mists began to thin until they could drop to eight hundred feet and still fly beneath an open, blue sky. Fog, however, still obscured the ocean surface, and although they were now above the patrol route of the submarine *Balilla*, their proximity could be confirmed only by radio.

As the hours passed, the planes' loads continued to lighten with the diminishing fuel supply, allowing greater agility and speed. The clouds and mists hanging low over the water broke up, and there, with its bells clanging and joyful whistle blasting streams of steam in the air, was the next support ship, the *Bigllieri*. On approach, the squadron decelerated and traced wide circles, dropping to a mere sixty feet over the ship's deck and masts, crowded with cap-waving, shouting sailors. Balbo and the ship's captain exchanged cheerful greetings by radio, and the flight resumed course.

Except for interspersions of low-lying clouds, the sky remained mostly clear, giving the aviators awe-inspiring views of icebergs, moody behemoths drifting silently and slowly from Arctic shelves. Then, amid the ice fields stretching to the western horizon came another great mass, at first barely detectable and then assuming an increasingly sharper and definite shape. That, affirmed Balbo's navigator, was the coast of Labrador. The air minister radioed his comrades, "Officers, non-commissioned officers, and airmen, I am in sight of the coast of Labrador. In a short time, our great task will be finished. Before we land, while our squadron still flies above the iceberg-strewn North Atlantic, I wish to convey to all of you my warmest congratulations. You will never forget the hardships encountered on this day, and neither will the Regia Aeronautica, which consecrates the task you have accomplished to our noble fatherland, and through it, the Duce. Long Live the King!"

With only a scattering of curious locals looking on, mostly indigenous fishermen, the layover at Cartwright took on the aspect of a college reunion aboard the awaiting *Alice*. In the company of only their ocean-borne comrades, they were met by none of the crowds and clamor that characterized the earlier layovers. As if by design, these proved to be the ideal circumstances for the aviators to unwind and relax after twelve hours and 1,500 harrowing miles of nonstop flight. A half-dozen Italian journalists had found their way to Cartwright but took care not to badger Balbo or the pilots with the usual flurry of questions and comment requests. Instead, the senior officers were invited to supper at the Grenfell Mission, a three-story frame building that served as one of the few medical clinics in the otherwise desolate region. A bottle of Grappa was uncorked, and the evening was spent singing together and trading jokes and stories.

Two days had been allowed for the stay at Cartwright, since it was speculated that the flying boats would need special attention after their grueling ocean hop. However, the mechanics found every component in perfect order during post-flight inspection and refueling. The next morning presented ideal flying conditions, so Balbo made the split decision to embark at once for the base at Shediac. Moving with their well-trained swiftness, the crews climbed in their planes and began the eight-hundred-mile trek at 8:30 a.m.

The Shediac layover was scheduled to be brief, with the Italians arriving late in the day and leaving first thing the following morning, but the residents of the seaside resort, chiefly famous for its lobster fisheries, had gone all out to receive them. Its streets were festooned with pennants, Italian flags and strings of colored lightbulbs, as well as a giant, illuminated display outlining the cruise's stopping points. The town's population of two thousand was supplemented by thirty thousand visitors, arriving by road and on special runs of the Canadian National Railroad dispatched specifically for the occasion. The unexpected decision to leave Cartwright a day ahead of schedule, however, threw the Shediac into chaos, as everyone rushed to finish preparations in time for the arrival. In fact, some of the key members of the welcoming committee, which included several Canadian government ministers and members of parliament, weren't even in town yet.

Not a single house or building was unvacated as masses of spectators crowded the shore to watch the air fleet's effortless descent on the tranquil waters of Shediac Bay. A phalanx of Mounties in their striking scarlet tunics stiffly saluted as Balbo and the other chief commanders stepped onto the wharf to booming applause.

Among the welcomers, Balbo recognized his twenty-four-year-old nephew Arcangelo, the son of his late brother Fausto. "Lino," as he was better known, was treated like a son by Balbo and his wife, Emanuella, after losing his father at the age of two. On leave from the army, he had traveled to Montreal to accompany his beloved uncle for a portion of the North American tour. A sharp crescendo in the cheers and clapping rose as the two rushed to embrace each other. Also present was journalist Nello Quilici, who had been running the *Corriere Padano* from the time Balbo had left Ferrara for a cabinet position in Rome. Another old face was the base commander Ernesto Campanelli; now a captain, he had been a simple sergeant-mechanic when he accompanied De Pinedo on the milestone Asian tour of 1925.

Again a series of salutations was given by the roster of dignitaries, and then Balbo was driven to the estate-like home of Dr. John Clarence Webster, at the time New Brunswick's most distinguished resident, where he enjoyed one of Shediac's world-renowned lobsters for dinner. He gratefully accepted the Webster family's invitation to spend the night, retiring early in quiet privacy to the comfortable suite prepared for him. The rest of the squadron dined and lodged at the Shediac Hotel and likewise chose to retreat to their beds for precious sleep before returning to the air in the morning.

The number of individuals flying in the squadron had increased to 117. Lino and Quilici were aboard I-BALB and several contingents of newsmen, technical specialists and diplomats were distributed aboard the other planes as the squadron left for the Montreal base at 8:30 a.m. As in the leg from Orbatello to Amsterdam, a good portion of the trip required miles of travel over dry land, always a bit unsettling for a flying boat, as the fleet cut northward six thousand feet above the thick forests of Maine to the St. Lawrence River. That much-traveled waterway would be the path to their next goal, which was reached at 1:00 p.m.

Balbo and Cagna spotted trouble waiting for them as soon as they began their descent. River traffic restrictions were either being ignored or unenforced, as evidenced by boats and launches skimming every which way near the landing zone. As their plane, first to alight as always, taxied toward the mooring basin, it nearly collided with a speeding motorboat bouncing its way directly toward their hull. The air minister watched in horror as other landing planes were forced to dodge or lift back off the water to avoid hitting the speedboats and launches that darted about the basin like bees around a hive.

For the first time of the entire enterprise, Balbo lost his composure, with the brunt of his ire aimed directly at base commander Captain Epifanio Del Ponte, who was just pulling up in a launch to transport him to shore. Launching into a profanity-sprinkled rebuke, Balbo demanded to know why the landing zone restrictions had not been enforced, ordering Del Ponte back to shore forthwith to do whatever it took to clear the landing and anchorage zones. Unfortunately, a reporter with a live microphone was also on Del Ponte's boat, and as Balbo later learned, to his total mortification, his entire tirade had been transmitted over local radio.

That awkward business aside, the reception given to the air fleet at Montreal vastly surpassed at any previous stop, although it was only a preview of what awaited the Italians in the near future. Police cars and motorcycles blared sirens and blasted horns as they gingerly cleared a path through thousands of spectators who blocked both sidewalk and streets for a glimpse of the *Atlantici* as they were led to the city's stately Mount Royal Hotel, at the time the largest in the whole of the British empire.

Here, as opposed to his short stopovers at Cartwright and Shediac, Balbo found no refuge from the teeming mob of newsmen and photographers, who angled, pushed and jostled to cluster immediately around him. They continued to cling to him the entire way to his hotel room, even waiting outside the bathroom into which Balbo retreated upon entering the suite. Finally conceding to the inevitable, he agreed to take questions in the hotel's dining room. Most of the newsmen sought details about the flight, of course, but almost as many of their questions were puzzling and even bizarre. One reporter asked him what his hobbies were, while another wanted to know why he sported a beard.

Such trivialities gradually reduced the interview to an exchange of good-natured banter, culminating with Balbo posing his own question regarding the number of journalists in Montreal. Given an estimate, roars of laughter rang through the hall when he replied that it would be so much more efficient if they could all be melted down to form one, single good reporter.

A five-hundred-plate dinner dance followed, prompting some mild consternation and embarrassment among its organizers when they belatedly realized that the main course of chicken would go untouched by many in attendance. It was a Friday, and the Italians, of course, were Catholics.

Excellent flying weather continued to hold, and the final lap of the inbound journey was expected to be reached with rapid ease as the crews boarded their machines the following morning. Several hours were lost, however, again clearing the takeoff lanes of boat traffic that had already returned to normal transport activities on the river. That difficulty surmounted, the squadron soared into the sky, pointing itself toward Chicago.

The scheduled flight path stretched westward over Lakes Huron and Erie, but reports were radioed that a treacherous storm had suddenly formed along the route, and Balbo was advised to make a detour. Circumventing the tempestuous weather meant entirely bypassing Lake Erie and cutting to the north.

After an hour, the squadron was skirting past Lake St. Clair and the mighty, smoke-spewing, industrial colossus of Detroit, where Balbo had been Henry Ford's guest back in 1929. The air fleet banked to the southwest, reaching Toledo at 3:40 p.m. Around this time, they were joined by three dozen U.S. Army pursuit planes, acting as an honor guard to escort them to Chicago's lakefront. South Bend was reached at 5:00 p.m. and, a few seconds later, New Buffalo on Lake Michigan's southwest shore. There, the crews spotted the gray, hazy outline of Chicago's skyline rising faint and low, but nonetheless distinguishable on the watery horizon.

CHICAGO

From northwest Indiana to Chicago's north suburbs, an estimated 1 million people had been jostling for a place along the Lake Michigan shoreline since morning on July 15, 1933, waiting to spot the squadron appear from the east. But it wasn't until 5:26 that afternoon that the planes were detected far off on the horizon.

The Italians reached the shoreline near 63rd Street on the South Side, traced a path to the North Side's Lawrence Avenue, turned west and then soared in a great circle above the city's inner neighborhoods, where thousands of residents filled the streets and climbed on the roofs of garages, houses and apartment buildings to get a better view of the flying boats, their silvery finishes gleaming in the late afternoon sun. Among the Chicagoans gazing upward from backyards, alleys and sidewalks was the city's future iconic mayor, Richard J. Daley, who, decades later, would recall, "All of us remember the beautiful day, the day they came out of the east…what a thrill! Every citizen of Chicago was electrified, regardless of his heritage."

Meanwhile, the army escort planes thrilled the crowds by positioning themselves to form the word *ITALY* before dispersing from the scene. Dozens of other private planes darted back and forth outside the squadron's flight path, and the Goodyear blimp and the dirigible *Macon* hovered above, while one of several more airships unfurled a long trailing banner that read "Hail Balbo and the Sons of Great Italy."

Banking to the east, the squadron began its descent on Lake Michigan in perfect order, gliding down on the water in groups of three to a deafening

Aerial view of the world's fair and SM-55X. *Joint Civic Committee of Italian Americans Collection (Chicago).*

cacophony of horns, bells, whistles, klaxons and the shouts and cheers of tens of thousands of spectators.

From their landing point across near Burnham Harbor, the flying boats taxied at greatly reduced speed to their mooring points on the north side of Navy Pier. The pilots stopped their engines, and the fleet came to rest, having logged 6,100 miles in the air. Although a welcoming party was standing by to greet Balbo aboard the USS *Wilmette*, the anchoring process moved with such caution that the final plane wasn't properly secured until 7:00 p.m. Only then were the Italians transported to the *Wilmette* on launches.

On board were Illinois governor Henry Horner, Chicago Mayor Edward Kelly, U.S. Federal World's Fair commissioner Henry S. New, President of the Century of Progress administration Rufus C. Dawes, U.S. Navy Admiral W.T. Cluvarius, U.S. Army Major Reed Landis and a dozen other dignitaries. But the first Americans Balbo met were reporters. The motorboat transporting him to the ship, he later remarked, was cornered nearly to the point of impassability by newsmen and photographers crowding about in every type of small vessel, snapping photos and shouting questions, some in broken Italian, that were virtually indecipherable due to the surrounding din. The air minister was, by now, well familiar with the persistence of the

Left: Arrival over Lake Michigan. *Joint Civic Committee of Italian Americans Collection (Chicago)*.

Below: Touching down on the water. *Joint Civic Committee of Italian Americans Collection (Chicago)*.

press, and since his stop in Montreal, he had developed a relationship with reporters often characterized by banter and good-natured humor. With a smile and wave, he simply shouted, "God Save America and God Save Italy!" in response to questions he really couldn't understand or even hear. There was no need for words in his next encounter, as his attention was drawn to another nearby boat just as his own had reached the *Wilmette*, this one crowded with young women who were waving and calling to him with

USS *Wilmette*. *Joint Civic Committee of Italian Americans Collection (Chicago)*.

great excitement. Balbo's already broad smile broadened further as he stood up in the boat and returned their greeting with a chivalrous bow.

A series of salvos and a nineteen-gun salute blasted from the *Wilmette* as the air minister and his *Atlantici* filed up the gangway. The originally planned formal reception and dinner aboard the ship had to be canceled due to the lateness of the hour, so after a flurry of introductions and handshakes, both hosts and guests reboarded the launches and were whisked to shore.

Incidentally, the *Wilmette* itself occupied its own storied place in Chicago's annals. Originally christened the *Eastland*, it regularly traversed the lake as an excursion ship from its date of construction in 1903 until July 24, 1915. On that horrifically fatal day, the top-heavy vessel spontaneously capsized in the Chicago River while taking on 2,500 Western Electric employees and their families bound for a company picnic in Michigan City, Indiana. Hundreds of passengers were trapped in submerged sections of the boat, and the resultant death toll of 844 souls went on record as the largest loss of life in any maritime incident on the Great Lakes. The *Eastland* was subsequently salvaged, purchased by the U.S. Navy and refitted as a gunboat as the rechristened USS *Wilmette*. Converted into a training vessel in 1941, the ship was decommissioned and scrapped after the Second World War.

A launch transports Balbo (fourth from left) and the welcoming committee from *Wilmette* to the fair. *Joint Civic Committee of Italian Americans Collection (Chicago).*

To the triumphal strains of Italian and American martial music rendered by several concert bands, the aviators and dignitaries climbed into a fifty-car cortege waiting off Burnham Harbor. The motorcade proceeded slowly, inching a path through thousands of cheering spectators held back by a phalanx of police and guardsmen, until it reached Soldier Field stadium at 8:30 p.m. With its Doric colonnades and Neoclassical lines, the stadium must have been reminiscent of Rome to the Italians, who were marched in to find it filled to capacity. A volcanic prolonged ovation exploded upon their entry. Balbo and his chief officers joined officials and dignitaries on a massive platform decorated in Italian and American colors. Towering loudspeakers were mounted both inside and outside the stadium so the tens of thousands who had been unable to secure a seat could listen in. National coverage of the welcoming ceremony was aired by Chicago's WGN radio, while the Italian consulate staff transmitted the proceedings to listeners in Italy.

When the applause quieted, Commissioner New, representing the federal government, opened the program with a congratulatory message to Balbo and his men from President Roosevelt. Governor Horner was next at the podium, followed by Kelly and Dawes. Then congratulatory messages by

Motorcade transports Decennale crew members through the fair. *Joint Civic Committee of Italian Americans Collection (Chicago).*

the U.S. secretaries of war and the navy were broadcast from Washington. Horner then took the podium, turned toward Balbo and said:

> *Mine is the honor of extending on behalf of the State of Illinois, sincere greetings and thrice hearty welcome to you and your squadron of gallant and heroic conquerors of the air. To this official salutation is added the enthusiastic congratulations of my fellow citizens and myself for the courageous, successful, and history-making flight you all have just completed.*
>
> *The occasion is epoch-making; it epitomizes dramatically and forcefully the progress of the world in the last one hundred years. Your daring and marvelous flight from Italy to Chicago marks another thrilling victory of man and science over the forces of nature and the passing of another milestone in the steady advance of air transportation.*
>
> *Just as Columbus was the first to sail the uncharted seas to our shores, so you, General Balbo, and your courageous band have piloted the first Armata*

Soldier Field. *Joint Civic Committee of Italian Americans Collection (Chicago).*

[sic] *of flying boats from Europe to North America. You have brought to us the living, emphatic proof of the development of practical aviation.*

Then, as if acclaiming the triumph of an ancient Roman general, Horner concluded, "All hail our distinguished visitors from Italy! All hail General Balbo, statesman, pioneer, hero, and apostle of the hour!"

After extending his own acclamations to the squadron, Mayor Kelly, next on the podium, made a surprise announcement. "Chicago realized the honor conferred upon her as the goal of this flight. The City Council has decreed that a thoroughfare leading to the Fairgrounds from our downtown streets shall be called Balbo Avenue!"

The air minister was particularly touched by this, one of dozens of honors that were showered on him over the weeks of the squadron's tour. This, he later said, unaware of the latter-day irony of the remark, would help preserve the memory of the Royal Italian Air Force and its great achievement forever in the minds of all Chicagoans.

Finally, Major Landis, chairman of the welcoming committee, took to the microphone and introduced the man of the hour, prompting yet another prolonged standing ovation. Balbo, bowing, with his natural broad and winning smile, made his way to the podium. Ambassador Rosso stood by adjacently with his own microphone to translate the air minister's words into English:

> *It is not possible to find the proper words to answer the distinguished gentlemen who have just spoken. We have today accomplished the mission entrusted to us by our chief. It is a message of friendship from the new Italy to the United States. There were many difficulties, but this welcome we are receiving is as much a reward as we could expect.*
>
> *Landing on American soil for the first time today, I wish to express on behalf of Fascist Italy the best wishes for your country, for your state, for your Fair, and for Chicago!*

When the ceremony ended, the dignitaries and their guests processed out of the stadium to a backdrop of triumphant music and sustained applause punctuated by repeated shouts of "Viva Balbo!" The scene was memorable enough for the Marx Brothers to mimic in their 1935 film *A Night at the Opera*, where they played a trio of uniformed foreign aviators being honored in New York to the strains of "Inno Di Garibaldi," a vigorous Italian march. Some of the performing bands at the fair that afternoon, incidentally, were local Italian ensembles, the type that were fixtures at the innumerable religious festivals held throughout the summer in Italian neighborhoods across the city and suburbs. Balbo's arrival, in fact, coincided with arguably the largest of these, the Feast of Our Lady of Mount Carmel, in the west suburban industrial town of Melrose Park. The Strocchia Band, one of Chicago's most prestigious of its genre, had been booked to play at both events, first to help welcome the *Atlantici* and later on the brilliantly illuminated bandstand at the Mount Carmel street festival. Under tight time pressure, Maestro Raffaele Strocchia labored strenuously to force his resistant ensemble, all young Italian musicians, onto a waiting streetcar and their next engagement. None of them, understandably, wanted to leave the once-in-a-lifetime event.

The motorcade was waiting to carry the *Atlantici* to their rooms at the Drake Hotel, and once everyone was situated, it slowly snaked its way along the three-mile route still jammed with cheering spectators. It was by now 10:00 p.m., and Balbo and his men, fairly exhausted, were relishing the thought of a good night's sleep in a comfortable bed. That inviting vision evaporated upon the discovery that a formal reception was waiting for them. All ninety-six officers and crew men, entering in small clusters, negotiated their way through the Drake's crowded lobby, nodding, smiling pleasantly and obliging constant requests for autographs. The reception, they further learned, was to be followed by a dinner dance that had been organized by a committee of ladies representing the cream of Chicago's High Society, and the surrounding profusion of flowers and decorations in the Italian colors hinted at the great deal of thought and expense that had gone into it. Although the aviators wanted nothing but rest, at least token attendance was clearly unavoidable.

Each man's personal baggage had been earlier delivered to his room, but in Balbo's suite, the first batch of hundreds of congratulatory telegrams from heads of state, government officials, aviation colleagues and celebrities pouring in from around the world had also arrived. Before heading to the night's festivities, he sat at the desk and composed cordial responses that were rushed to the hotel's Western Union office. At 11:30 p.m., two airmen, now in immaculate white dress uniforms, shyly entered the reception hall almost entirely unnoticed by the roomful of smartly attired occupants, mingling and chatting with one another. After silently appraising the buffet table's small tea sandwiches, the two inched their way directly into the hotel's adjoining dining room. There they found six of their companions already seated, scarfing down huge steaks, their first taste of food for the day.

The dinner dance was held at the Saddle & Cycle Club, a private recreational center on Chicago's posh north shore. On each table were red and white ribbons, intermingled with green, arranged in the shape of an airplane. Along with those of the Italian guests, place cards bore the names of Governor Horner, Prince Potenziani, Ambassador Rosso, Consul General Castruccio and their wives, as well as dozens of high civilian and military officials expected to attend. Prominent settings were prepared for guests representing Chicago's most illustrious families—the Palmers, McCormicks and Armours among them—strategically placed near to those of Balbo's top officers.

It wasn't until after midnight that Balbo and a contingent of his officers entered the door, and due to the late hour, the place settings of many of the invitees remained unused. The standard series of welcoming orations was cut short, and first courses had been barely consumed before the orchestra signaled the start of the post-dinner dance. Already having relaxed his normally strict bedtime orders, Balbo allowed those of his men who had not yet retired to enjoy themselves on the dance floor in the company of the pretty debutantes fawning over them.

Predictably, the activities planned for Sunday morning had to be crossed off the day's schedule of events. Balbo had promised his men that they could sleep in. The program, then, didn't begin until noon and High Mass, celebrated by Cardinal Mundelein at Holy Name Cathedral. Forty thousand Chicagoans were already gathering inside and on the blocks surrounding the church when the motorcade arrived, while four hundred Chicago policemen, mounted and on foot, strained to maintain order and clear a path to the entrance. They were already almost a half hour late. Mayor Kelly, already in a pew with his wife, later quipped to reporters that this was the first time in his knowledge that the cardinal had ever delayed the commencement of High Mass at the cathedral.

Balbo, his chief officers and pilots wore crisply pressed, brilliantly white uniforms, white kid gloves on their hands, their white shoes buffed and polished. The noncommissioned officers wore the standard regulation dress blues of the *Regia Aeronautica*. Subdued applause played around them as they marched up the stone steps, giving way to the solemnly muted tones of the cathedral organ once they passed into the cool, incense- and blossom-scented dimness of the church's interior. Thick profusions of flowers decorated the

Aviators at Holy Name Cathedral. *Joint Civic Committee of Italian Americans Collection (Chicago).*

Crowds outside church. *Joint Civic Committee of Italian Americans Collection (Chicago).*

majestic High Altar, and candles and vigil lamps flickered everywhere amid gleaming marble.

Hats removed, Balbo and all of his ninety-six companions lined up into the front rows of pews. There they stood, stiff and motionless as statues for the entirety of the holy services. Their only movements came when, at the appropriate times, they bowed their heads or made the Sign of the Cross. So impressive was this display of rigid discipline that *Tribune* reporter James Bennet inadvertently exposed the Anglo American–held stereotypes of the era by remarking that many of Balbo's men looked more like young Englishmen rather than Italians.

Benediction followed Mass, and after that a message transmitted from the Vatican was read, in which the pope congratulated the squadron and assured the aviators of his prayers for a safe return home.

After the recessional, all parties rendezvoused at the fair for a formal luncheon in the palatial Hall of Sciences, a lengthy, speech-laden affair that did not finish up until 4:00 p.m. Stepping out into the warm, late afternoon sunshine, Balbo and his chief officers strolled the short distance to the

Italian pavilion, while noncoms dispersed into the fairgrounds. Mounting a speaker's platform in the building's reception hall and with Consul General Castruccio translating, Balbo gave an account of the flight and offered his thoughts on the challenges and possibilities of transcontinental aviation to a select audience of about one hundred dignitaries, concluding by once more expressing his deep gratitude for Chicago's extraordinary hospitality.

Back outside, American military planes saluted the Italians with a spectacular aerobatic show over the lake. Then, with evening approaching, there was just enough time to drive back to the Drake and enjoy a brief rest and freshen up in preparation of their next celebratory banquet, this time hosted by the leaders of Chicago's Italian American community, with Cook County judge John Sbarbaro as its coordinator. Held at the Stevens Hotel, guests at the five-thousand-plate affair dined to a medley of popular Italian melodies and operatic transcriptions performed by an ensemble from Chicago's Civic Opera Orchestra. Once the tables were cleared, the familiar stream of tributes were bestowed on Balbo, his officers and their crews by a succession of distinguished speakers. An honorary science degree was conferred on the Italian air minister by Reverend Robert Kelley, president of Loyola University, and all of his flyers were awarded official American pilot licenses. Commemorative plaques and ribboned tributes were presented at the conclusion of each of the many speeches by representatives of the civic, religious and professional organizations in attendance.

William Washburn Child, the former U.S. ambassador to Italy, read a message from President Roosevelt: "I request that you express to General Balbo and his gallant companions my profound admiration and my sincere congratulations upon the triumphal success of their transatlantic flight. The enterprise, which has upon it the stamp of thorough scientific preparation, marks an important step in the conquest of the air. Please convey to them my greetings."

Balbo himself was finally called to the podium. He began by introducing his airmen in roll call fashion, during which, upon hearing his name, each man stood up at attention and shouted back "*Presente!*" The entire squadron sprang to its feet when he reached the name of Sergeant Ugo Quintavalle, the crewman tragically killed in Amsterdam, their combined voices thundering "*Presente!*" to honor their fallen comrade.

Balbo proceeded by describing the depth of pride he held for his *Atlantici*. Their skill, courage, sharp minds and steady hands were the primary reason behind the success of the Decennale cruise. Likewise, he went on, the millions of Italians who had immigrated to America, the parents or

Stevens Hotel banquet. *Joint Civic Committee of Italian Americans Collection (Chicago).*

individuals themselves, many of whom had just now broken bread with him in the banquet hall, had amply demonstrated their own endurance, persistence and courage which merited no less admiration. They should never be embarrassed by their foreign origins, he asserted, but instead take pride in the way their honest toil has so greatly contributed to the growth of their adopted homeland.

The following morning's crowded agenda began with a tour of Chicago Municipal Airport (later named Midway Airport), which having handled more than sixty thousand commercial and airmail flights the previous year had already secured the title of world's busiest. The visit naturally piqued Balbo's interest perhaps more than any other of the many scheduled events for his brief stay in the city, and he carefully inspected the facility's layout and observed its operations. As he had noted during his first trip to the United States in 1929 and would frequently mention in later recollections of the 1933 cruise, Americans seemed to do everything on a grand scale, colossal when compared to Europe—skyscrapers, streets, bridges, railroads, factories and airports. No country could rival it now, nor probably ever in the future.

Mayor Kelly presents the Key to Chicago. *Italian Air Force Historical Office.*

Next on the schedule was a brief stop at city hall, where the Key to the City was ceremoniously handed to Balbo by Mayor Kelly, followed by a drive to the intersection of Michigan Blvd and 7th Street for the unveiling of the new street sign bearing the air minister's name. Then the entire party traveled a few blocks south to witness the dedication of the towering Columbus statue, which, like the street, would be the source of so much controversy decades later.

Afterward, the *Atlantici* split into two groups and headed off in different directions. Balbo and the pilots went back to the Drake to review the next leg of their journey, while the flight engineers and noncoms were driven to Navy Pier. There they donned overhauls and spent the rest of the day inspecting and tuning up the aircraft engines while hundreds of curious spectators looked on.

Later that afternoon, Balbo and his officers were at the fair again and guided to its Indian Village for a demonstration of traditional dances by members of the Sioux Nation in full regalia. Arms crossed, two stern-faced chieftains named Black Thorn and Evergreen Tree stood silent and erect amid the rhythmic chanting and throbbing drums. At a culminating point, the dancing and tom toms abruptly ceased, and Black Horn strode up to Balbo, took him by the hand and led him to the middle of the performance area. There, Evergreen Tree solemnly crowned him with an enormous eighty-feathered headdress, announcing the air minister's formal induction into the tribe as "Chief Flying Eagle." One of the most photographed events of the visit, the massive, surrounding crowd cheered and applauded as Balbo, smiling with delight, posed in his new and colorful garb.

All of the crewmen reunited that evening for the next banquet, this one offered by the U.S. government at the Congress Hotel. Afterward, a portion

Balbo Avenue
unveiled. *Italian Air
Force Historical Office.*

of those in attendance followed the *Atlantici* to the exclusive Casino Club, a private restaurant and ballroom popular with the most fashionable Chicago socialites. Here the night would close with another formal reception and dance. This white tie event was again organized by a committee of wealthy Chicago matrons in coordination with Prince Potenziani. Those included on the very select list of invitees enjoyed an opportunity to shake Balbo's hand and share a few cordial words with him as they made their way down the receiving line.

The ball began at midnight. At the tables surrounding the dance floor, all of the airmen were joined by dance partners, elegantly gowned, young, single women from socially prominent families. An hour later—and against the backdrop of tangos, waltzes, laughter and cheerful conversation—Balbo leaned over and whispered something to Major Landis, with whom he was

Balbo inducted into the Sioux Tribe as "Chief Flying Eagle." *Joint Civic Committee of Italian Americans Collection (Chicago).*

sharing a table. At the major's signal, a few other gentlemen joined in hushed conversation until several of them nodded and left the room. A few minutes later, one reappeared and gave another nod, and Balbo, Landis and six other guests quietly rose and slipped out the door.

94

The group of eight, four men and four women, climbed into a waiting car and then drove off to the nearby Drake Hotel. Balbo hurriedly entered and soon rejoined his companions in a dark, civilian suit, the brim of a hat pulled slanted and low over his eyebrows. At the club, he had confessed to Landis his yearning to see the Midway, the fair's vibrant amusement park, which had caught his eye but had no opportunity to visit. Landis and a select handful of socialites were obliging that desire. The party was soon strolling amid the brilliantly illuminated attractions of the Midway, but with the formal attire of Balbo's companions undermining the plot to remain inconspicuous.

One of the first amusements they chose were the bumper cars. Each member of the group climbed into an electrically powered, miniature car and, laughing and hooting, proceeded to glide around in great circles to collide and ram into one another. After that, Balbo tried his hand at a shooting gallery and several ball tossing games before enjoying a 3.2 beer, as Prohibition was still in force, under the festive strings of market lights of the Midway's beer garden.

Someone with the party suggested a stop at the Pirate Ship, a nightclub-like concession where the famously rambunctious entertainer Texas Guinan and her dance troupe were performing. Guinan had finished the set just as the group stepped in the door, and Balbo mistook the ensuing applause as a sign that he had been recognized. Wanting a break from the constant cheering and accolades, he instinctively spun around and hurried back outside. Except for that brief encounter, he was certain that his escapade at the Midway had passed unnoticed. Not until the next day did Balbo learn that sharp-eyed reporters had been trailing him from the moment his party had scurried out of the Casino Club, with the morning newspapers reporting his every move at Midway.

Once again, the excessively late bedtimes for Balbo and most of his men meant a sluggish start to the scheduled activities for July 18, their last full day in Chicago. Morning events were canceled, and the program didn't get underway until noon with a formal luncheon sponsored by U.S. Army and Navy officers at the Stevens Hotel. There, Admiral Cluverius took yet another opportunity to raise a toast to the flyers with a brief philosophical observation that modern sources continue to erroneously attribute to American tennis star Andre Ashe. "Success is a journey, not a destination," the admiral intoned, further proclaiming his confidence that Italy would not remain still after this latest aerial triumph.

Balbo and his pilots were back in their motorcade by 2:30 p.m. to proceed with the next of the day's events, while his noncoms were granted leave for

State Street parade. *From* Cieli E Mari *(1973).*

the afternoon to freely roam about the fair. Escorted by a mounted platoon of U.S. cavalry, the town cars paraded down Michigan Avenue, moving at a crawl while their occupants waved cheerfully to the applauding masses who lined the road fifteen deep or leaned out from the windows of virtually every one of the surrounding buildings for fourteen blocks.

Reaching the Chicago River, the cavalrymen positioned themselves to the sides and drew their sabers in salute while the motorcade crossed the bridge and began the seventeen-mile trip north to Fort Sheridan, a U.S. Army post on the Lake Michigan shoreline. The parade grounds at the fort had been opened to the public, and an estimated ten thousand local spectators, the largest crowd to assemble there since World War I, turned out to welcome the Italians. Festivities opened with a review of parading American troops and another American military air show. Balbo's officers were subsequently invited to join their American counterparts in a polo match, and the visit wrapped up with another formal reception.

A detour was made on the way back so that Balbo and his men could visit Columbus Hospital, built in 1905 by St. Francis Xavier Cabrini and operated by the Missionary Sisters of the Sacred Heart of Jesus. Almost all of the nuns were of Italian background, and the smooth fluidity of their native language rolled through the halls and corridors as they easily conversed with their visitors. Each of the aviators was given a silver rose as a memento, with Balbo receiving an extra three of them for his children.

At his request, that evening's usual line schedule of busy activities was substituted by a quiet, private dinner at Chicago's Tavern Club Restaurant. His men, he explained, had to be up and ready to depart before the coming dawn.

Indeed, at 5:30 a.m. the following morning, hotel servers were rolling food carts down the Drake's halls, knocking on doors and presenting each of the airmen with a light breakfast of orange juice, coffee and toast. Suitcases were gathered on luggage carts and transported to Navy Pier along with the mechanics who engaged in the last-minute inspection checks and takeoff preparations. Even at that early hour, several thousand

General Balbo. *Joint Civic Committee of Italian Americans Collection (Chicago).*

Chicagoans had shown up to watch the departure. By the time of takeoff, that number had increased to 100,000 spectators on or around the pier and other stretches of the lakefront.

Just before 8:00 a.m., the first group of the planes taxied from the mooring basin to the delineated takeoff path on the open lake. Once their powerful engines had lifted them off the water, they soared upward and traced large circles over the fair until the rest of the squadron, in sequence, joined them in the air. The *Wilmette*, anchored nearby, fired another nineteen cannon blasts in a farewell salute, and again a squadron on American military planes flew in to escort the departing flying boats, which, having positioned themselves in proper formation, gradually vanished in the eastern horizon.

As a side note, while Chicago had been outdoing itself to celebrate its guests, the residents of another Midwest town were looking on with more than a little envy and disappointment. Major Tempesti was well aware that conditions on the Great Lakes could quickly turn harsh. Storms were known to rise with little warning to produce waves as high as twenty feet. As his fellow chief officers at the stopover points had done, he sought an alternate landing point on the outside chance that weather conditions precluded a safe descent upon the squadron's arrival. He zeroed in on Wisconsin's placid, eight-square-mile Lake Geneva, a crystal-clear, freshwater remnant of the receding glaciers of the last ice age, just over the Illinois border about eighty miles north of Chicago. Its surrounding town, also named Lake Geneva, developed as a tranquil resort community after wealthy Chicagoans started building summer homes along the water in the late nineteenth century.

The prospect of their lake serving as an alternate landing point was received quite favorably by municipal authorities and owners of the town's mostly tourist-oriented businesses, and permission to use it as such was promptly transmitted to the Italian Air Ministry. Enthusiasm further intensified at the approach of flight's launching date, when Tempesti's ground crew arrived to fix mooring buoys with squadron flag markers at carefully measured positions in the lake.

Despite the high improbability of the squadron needing to ever use the buoys or any other facilities there, the residents of Lake Geneva seemed to talk themselves into believing Balbo's visit was a certainty, if not as a contingency then as a part of his local itinerary while in Chicago. Through social connections and diplomatic channels, the town's most influential citizens succeeded in having a tentative flight to Lake Geneva included on the squadron's schedule.

A welcoming committee was organized, the streets were decorated with flags and ribbons and the usual sumptuous banquet was planned. Chicago newspapers booked rooms for reporters at the town's largest hotel, and Chicago leading radio stations, WBBM and WGN, set up temporary radio stations to transmit live broadcasts of the occasion. A short-wave radio station was placed on the hotel's top floor to communicate directly with the Italian pilots and guide them in.

Measures were worked out for crowd control with the expectation that thousands of spectators from the surrounding townships would be descending on the streets and parkways surrounding the lake for a glimpse of the flying boats and their crews. Lake Geneva's tiny police and fire departments were supplemented by volunteers from the local American Legion and a contingent of sixty U.S. Army troops dispatched from Fort Sheridan. After Consul General Castruccio's receipt of bomb threats, Tempesti requested and was granted even greater security provided in the form of a detachment of the Wisconsin National Guard.

The squadron's trouble-free landing in Chicago deprived Lake Geneva of attaining even a modest degree of worldwide attention as a contingency landing point. Lingering hopes of hosting the squadron in any case were reduced to profound disappointment when Balbo cabled, "I know wonderful preparations have been arranged by the people of Lake Geneva to receive us. With much regret and on account of official reasons, I'm sorry to be unable to visit the city that has done all in its power to prepare the base for our fleet.…I extend to your committee and the generous people of Lake Geneva my cordial regrets."

As a consolation prize, Colonel Carlo Tempesti, one of Balbo's ground crew officers, who arrived in town to collect the buoys and mooring gear, instead gifted them to the town as souvenirs of an event that might have been.

WASHINGTON, D.C., NEW YORK AND THE CONCLUSION

The American escort dispersed over Toledo, and Balbo led his planes across Lake Erie, allowing the crews to enjoy a spectacular aerial view of Niagara Falls before banking southeast toward New York City. Climbing to twelve thousand feet, the planes tightened formation in their diagonal crossing of the state and then descended cautiously as they approached the sprawling metropolitan region. In an era before air traffic control, Balbo's chief concern was the uncomfortable number of other planes maneuvering to get as close as possible so the newsmen on board could photograph the Italian fleet.

The Hudson River was reached at 6:45 p.m., and the squadron followed its Manhattan shoreline and then turned eastward to New York Harbor, where, to the aviators' delight, they spotted the majestic *Rex*, a massive Italian tricolor on its stern and its decks packed with waving, shouting spectators and sailors. The Italian liner greeted the seaplanes by blasting its thunderous horn. The flyers later recalled that it was barely distinguishable, since every other vessel in the harbor, whether ship or boat, whether docked or sailing, was also sounding sirens, bells and whistles to hail the squadron's arrival.

The planes continued their slow descent by circumnavigating the city, passing by the Statue of Liberty, the Brooklyn Bridge and then the neighborhoods where, as in Chicago, streets, alleys and rooftops were jammed with hundreds of thousands of local residents, all heads turned to the sky and arms exuberantly waving. Finally, at 8:00 p.m., the flying boats began alighting on the waters of Jamaica Bay for mooring at the shoreline of Floyd Bennett Airfield. The one-thousand-mile journey had taken seven hours and six minutes.

With the planes secured, Balbo and his men were greeted on shore by a welcoming party headed by New York publisher Generoso Pope, federal and local government officials and, to the aviators' happy surprise, world heavyweight boxing champion Primo Carnera. Accompanied by several hundred motorcycle policemen, a motorcade carrying the aviators penetrated its way along the twelve-mile route to Park Avenue's Ambassador Hotel down streets densely packed with cheering New Yorkers, beneath lampposts and buildings thickly decorated with the Italian colors.

Upon arrival at the hotel, Balbo was presented with a telegram from Charles Lindbergh and his wife, Anne, at the moment in Newfoundland as part of an aerial survey of the North Atlantic they had been hired to conduct for Pan American Airways: "Please accept our warm congratulations on your splendid flight. You have given an example of excellent organization put into effect with marvelous precision. We regret exceedingly that we were unable to meet you at Cartwright, but we are very glad to have met your fellow officers of the Alice."

Balbo answered immediately, remarking how flattered he and all his *Atlantici* were to receive recognition from the man he described as "America's most brilliant hero" and concluding by wishing Lindbergh many future aerial triumphs.

The next morning, Balbo was expected to be in Washington, D.C., in response to President Franklin Delano Roosevelt's request to meet him personally. Deeply honored, he naturally wanted to be at his best for the occasion and, being well fatigued from his seven-hour nonstop fight, hoped for a solid night's sleep. But again this hope was sabotaged upon learning that he was to be the guest of honor at a welcoming banquet not set to begin until 9:00 p.m. at the Columbia Yacht Club. Since New York governor Herbert Lehman, Mayor John P. O'Brien and other dignitaries would be present, Balbo was obligated to attend. As it happened, he enjoyed the affair, particularly when O'Brien, a Democrat, and U.S. Army General Dennis Nolan, a Republican, competed in a lighthearted attempt at persuading Balbo to stay in the United States and run for political office on their respective party tickets.

Mere hours later, guest services personnel at the Ambassador were gently knocking on the hotel room doors of Balbo and two dozen officers, a predawn courtesy wakeup call and reminder that taxis were waiting to bring them to the airport. Weary and sluggish, they showered, dressed and were shuttled back to Bennet Field, where a small fleet of military aircraft waited to fly them to Washington.

Balbo in Washington. *National Archives and Records Administration.*

Balbo seized the opportunity to grab some sleep for the short duration of the flight. He had only a few minutes to compose himself when he was awakened by attendants as the plane descended on Bolling Field in Washington, D.C. *Marcia Reale* (Royal March), the spirited and exuberant Italian national anthem, was struck by the U.S. Navy Band as Balbo made his way down the runway stairs, his gaze turning to survey the thirty thousand highly animated citizens who had come out to see him.

The air minister and his officers stood at attention as the traditional nineteen-gun salute was fired, the band continuing to deliver ruffles and flourishes. The Italians were then formally welcomed to the capital by U.S. secretaries of commerce, navy and war. A young woman handed Balbo a wreath of flowers, and then everyone climbed aboard another motorcade and drove to the Mayflower Hotel.

Directed to their suites, the Italians had about an hour to freshen up before resuming a day crowded with activities. Some, including Balbo, sent their uniforms down to be cleaned and pressed and their shoes polished. Others simply requested cups of coffee.

The airmen not visiting the White House were invited to a luncheon and a program of musical entertainment offered at the hotel by the Overseas

Writers Club, an association of journalists and foreign correspondents. Afterward, local radio stations aired interviews with the pilots, who gave listeners their accounts of the flight and their impressions of America and New York City.

Accompanying Balbo to the White House were his staff officers Pellegrino, Cagna and Longo. Reporters and photographers were not allowed at the presidential luncheon, so details on what transpired were available only through the accounts of those in attendance. Before making their way to the dining hall, Balbo and his officers were introduced to Roosevelt in the White House Blue Room, a traditional reception hall for distinguished guests. Balbo smiled with surprise and appreciation when, while shaking his hand, the president spoke to him in Italian. It was one of several languages in which Roosevelt could get by passably if not fluently. Each of the guests was greeted in the same manner, and after some light conversation, everyone was directed to the dining hall. Cabinet officials, army and navy officers, Ambassador Rosso and Italian military attachés were seated at round banquet tables, each bearing a centerpiece of fragrant roses. Balbo, of course, shared his table with the president. Conversation, he remarked afterward, was constant and pleasant.

"Like all Americans, the President is a man of extraordinary courtesy and genial, easy manner. Not for one moment during the luncheon did the president fail to rivet my earnest attention and that of the guests with his animated conversational power. I felt all the time that I was in the presence of a statesman of enormous breadth of vision and tireless energy."

Roosevelt later presented Balbo with an elaborately bound album with the request that it be returned to the White House with the autographs of every one of the ninety-six participants in the Decennale cruise. The request, which Balbo interpreted to mean the American president shared with him mutual admiration and respect for the crew, was happily honored.

From the White House, Balbo and his staff were joined by their comrades at Arlington Cemetery, and there he solemnly placed a massive wreath on the Tomb of the Unknown Soldier. The Italians, resembling American navy officers in their immaculately white uniforms, saluted stiffly as the bugle played taps. A brief trip to the Lincoln Memorial followed, and then all of the officers and pilots gathered at the Italian embassy for a reception hosted by Rosso, where they were introduced to other foreign ambassadors and officials.

The activities wrapped up with a banquet and ball at the Army-Navy Country Club, a gala affair attended by top-ranking military personnel,

General Douglas MacArthur among them; congressmen and their spouses; and the usual members of the district's glittering upper class. After dinner, a progression of speakers conveyed the by now familiar stream of accolades, the inevitable comparisons between Balbo and Columbus, protestations of the tight bonds of friendship between Italy and the United States and praise for the scrupulous preparations behind the Decennale's success.

When the dance portion of the evening began, Balbo was interviewed by the National Broadcasting Network, airing live across the country. When asked through an interpreter about what his Atlantic cruise had accomplished, Balbo modestly replied, "We have only demonstrated that what a few have done, great numbers will be doing through the safety of systematic operations."

The aviators returned to the Mayflower after the dance, but not for the good night's sleep they had so far been denied. To accommodate the vast number of scheduled events waiting for them, they had to get back to New York immediately. This time, though, they would be traveling by train, which meant a longer ride, which, thankfully, meant a better chance of a few more hours of rest. Minutes after their train departed at 2:30 a.m., the Italians were sound asleep.

Since the first activity of the day didn't start until late morning, the men enjoyed the luxury of a few extra hours of undisturbed peace at the Ambassador. Then, awakening to a light breakfast, they once again donned their dress uniforms and boarded a cortege of forty open-topped cars for a ticker-tape parade down Broadway. According to police estimates reported in the *Washington Post*, an incredible 2 million New Yorkers flooded the streets for a glimpse of Balbo and the crews, who waved back, all smiles but a bit mystified by the rainstorm of tiny strips of paper drifting down on them. Balbo, curiously, picked one up and studied it meticulously in a vain attempt to decipher the tiny stock exchange–marked letters and numbers printed on it.

Military marches echoed in the urban canyons formed by mammoth skyscrapers, their gallant notes mingling with sirens, steam whistles, bells and the applause and cheers emulating from a million throats. The scene stretched all the way to city hall, where the parade terminated, and its honorees were escorted to the city council assembly room in which nearly one thousand spectators were already crammed. Mayor O'Brien opened the proceedings by presenting Balbo with a gold medal bearing the seal of New York City, its reverse side featuring an engraving of two clasped hands under the words "Italy."

This sentiment of international friendship was the focus of his subsequent speech and the flight's role in strengthening it:

> *That your entire fleet of twenty four airplanes should have arrived here safely and in such perfect order was the cause of thankfulness on the part of all of us and a source of both amazement and wonder. The daring of it, the perfection of organization involved, the skill and perseverance which it betokens on the part of every one of you caused a real heart throb to every citizen of this city.*
>
> *As one witness to your great flight down the Hudson River on Wednesday afternoon, I could not but reflect on the possible meaning of it all. Could such perfection of invention become instruments of warfare and be instrumental in the destruction of civilization? I am sure that you will agree with me that the effort of every nation should be centered around the prevention of any such possibility. But as messengers of peace and goodwill as instruments of commerce and transportation. What amazing possibilities lie before us!*

Thomas A. Morgan, representing the Aeronautical Chamber of Commerce of America, continued on a similar note when he declared from the podium, "Your flight marks the beginning of another era in man's conquest of the air; an era when all people of the Earth, because of speed which flying gives over land and sea will be united by a common bond of fast transportation to live as brothers in mutual understanding and perfect peace," according to the *Christian Science Monitor*.

Balbo responded in his now familiar fashion that he himself was "not entitled" to the lavish accolades, directing instead the Decennale's success to its crewmen, planners and ground support personnel. But he emphasized his wholehearted agreement in the hope that the chief accomplishment of the flight would be the promotion of international peace and friendship.

Madison Square Garden was next on the agenda, an event that was organized when Balbo, prior to his New York arrival, was handed the list of activities being planned for him there. A two-week stay would not be possible to accommodate them all, he declared, and he subsequently messaged the Italian consul general in New York asking if it was possible to consolidate them in a single venue. As a result, the members of a multitude of Italian American social and fraternal groups, institutional organizations and similar entities that had invited Balbo and his men to their respective banquets and receptions instead assembled at the city's famous arena.

The ceremony there was broadcast by radio both nationally and in Italy. Not one seat or standing space was unfilled when the air minister and his airmen reached the famous stadium, and a deafening, prolonged blend of applause, cheers and shouts roared from an audience seventy thousand strong upon spotting their entry. Since the majority of those present were from New York's vast Italian American population, it was to them that Balbo addressed his remarks from the speaker's stand.

Focusing on a subject that only they could fully appreciate, he assured them that he was fully mindful of not only the material hardships endured by those of his "race and faith" who had come to America, but also their spiritual sufferings, the social debasement they had faced as lowly immigrants in new, unfamiliar land so culturally different from their own.

"Take pride in the fact that you are Italians!" he declared, promising that, thanks to the policies of Mussolini and the Fascist regime, the painful era of humiliation was over. And with that, they, too, had a role to play as representatives of a new and vigorous Italy, with the duty of contributing toward the advancement of civilization through diligent and honest labor. While they should never detach themselves from their ancestral roots, they must always honor their adopted land, respect its laws and revere the glorious star-spangled banner as much as they would the Italian tricolor. "Forever may they wave side by side and may nothing separate them!"

Like the earlier scene at Soldier Field, a flourish of Italian and American patriotic music accompanied Balbo and his men as they left the arena and back to their hotel through streets still crowded with admirers. After a short rest there, the rather strenuous schedule continued with dinner at the Commodore Hotel, then a gigantic reception and ball at the opulent Waldorf Astoria. The night unfolded with yet another repetition of the standard program of distinguished speakers lavishing praise on Balbo and the *Atlantici* in a cavernous ballroom filled with three thousand of New York's most illustrious and prominent citizens. As the night progressed and attention turned toward the dance floor, Balbo, in a close replication of the events at the Stevens Hotel banquet in Chicago, quietly expressed to Ambassador Rosso his long-held wish to visit the press rooms of the *New York Times*, a desire born out of his own journalist days. In short order, the air minister and a small accompaniment of other banquet guests climbed into a taxi and were on their way to that destination.

The plant manager was alerted of their coming, and a tour was given of the massive labyrinth of rotary presses, linotype machines and conveyor systems loudly churning out the next morning editions of the *Times*. Balbo

Balbo in New York. *Italian Air Force Historical Office.*

was enthralled by the sheer size of the mammoth yet smoothly flowing process, enforcing his conviction of the unequaled ingenuity and power of American industry. As the entourage made its way among the machines, Balbo was delighted to discover a large number of Italians among the equipment operators. Exchanging greetings in their native language, he inquired about their jobs, and one of them even allowed Balbo to try his hand at a linotype machine. "There is no American enterprise," he later wrote, "in which the ingenuity of our people is not engaged."

Once again, neither Balbo nor any of his men went to bed before 2:00 a.m., and before doing so they requested not to be disturbed until long after the sun had risen. No one knocked on his door until 1:00 p.m., when he opened it to find the hall outside filled with patiently waiting newsmen. He invited the reporters to join him for a late breakfast, and it would be there that, with the help of a translator, he would answer their questions.

The interview stretched over a range of topics: the route for return flight home, its anticipated challenges, the surface support apparatus and specifically its communication system. From the latter topic, the discussion drifted to his direct communications with Italy during the entire journey. At that, Balbo revealed that his most regular contact with home were the daily phone calls he made to his wife. Excusing himself from the table, Balbo reminded the reporters of his hope that he and his men could spend the remainder of their visit in New York free of the continuous, frenzied activity they had so far experienced. They sincerely appreciated all the attention, he stressed, but were in serious need of rest.

From there, he retired back to his room, spending the next several hours reviewing weather reports, maps and route options with Pellegrino and the squadron leaders. That evening, they all enjoyed a quiet dinner at the private suburban home of Mr. and Mrs. Morton Schwartz, prominent socialites whom they had met during their stay in Chicago, while the other crewmen dined at the hotel or enjoyed local fare at nearby restaurants.

Every crewman got a full, uninterrupted night's repose, and their countenances were much less strained and weary when they all attended Mass at St. Patrick's Cathedral the following Sunday morning. Again, Balbo and his staff accepted an invitation for lunch at the Long Island country estate of another wealthy couple, free from teeming crowds, photographers and reporters. As usual, the noncoms and mechanics headed back to the mooring point to prep the planes for the next stage of the journey.

Balbo returned to the thick of things later that afternoon when he made a special trip to New York's Roosevelt Hotel to call on American aviator Wiley Post, freshly back in town from an eight-day solo flight around the world. Balbo could move about a bit more freely since Post was now the center of media attention. The American flyer recognized Balbo instantly when Balbo entered the hotel's reception hall, and a sense of camaraderie developed just as quickly. The air minister listened intently as Post, tired but cheerful, answered his inquiries about the technical and logistical details of the fifteen-thousand-mile trip.

Newsmen hastened to position the two men in front of a barrage of microphones to capture their exchange. With his eye patch and blunt, rough-around-the-edges mannerisms, Post contrasted sharply with Balbo's smooth and polished demeanor. Post momentarily stunned reporters when he spouted, "I think most generals are phony!" Then, after a brief pause, he looked directly at Balbo and continued, "But you have absolutely proved yourself to be a General to have gone out and taken charge of such a flight as you have made!"

The two aviators traded more compliments, shook hands and gave each other hearty pats on the back, with Balbo then stepping off to turn the attention of the press fully back on Post.

With departure scheduled for dawn, every airman was ordered to be back in his hotel room by 8:00 p.m. The next morning, however, heavy fog blanketed the landing point at Shediac, the first layover station en route home. Four hours passed waiting in vain for news that conditions had improved; consensus was reached among Balbo and the squadron leaders to postpone takeoff until the following day. The remainder of the afternoon was spent mostly back at the Ambassador, although some killed time by strolling the surrounding Manhattan avenues. It was now just a normal Monday morning in New York City. The thousands who had so energetically cheered the *Atlantici* were back at work, and life had snapped back to normal. Now they could all observe the busily humming metropolis function in its truest daily form. Balbo himself took the opportunity of unscheduled free time to chat on the phone with his wife and children; then, along with Pellegrini, he left his room to ride an elevator to the top of the Empire State Building, marveling at the breathtaking views.

CURIOUSLY, DURING THE ENTIRETY of the squadron's sojourn there, Francesco de Pinedo was also in New York, traveling under the alias of "Mr. Brown." Chafing from being grounded and isolated, he had retired from the *Regia Aeronautica* with the intent of returning to the air as a civilian and to do so in a big way. He kept his profile low while purchasing and modifying a Bellanca monoplane at his own expense, planning to use it to set a new world record by flying nonstop from New York to Baghdad. Despite his attempt at anonymity, his presence was rooted out by vigilant newsmen. To their inquiries on his motive, the forty-two-year-old De Pinedo answered, "I want to find out how old I am," according to the *New York Times*.

He shared a few more light comments with reporters before climbing into the cockpit at New York's Bennet Field began just before sunrise on September 3. A few minutes later, the Bellanca, loaded with more than one thousand gallons of fuel, was accelerating for takeoff when it unexpectedly swerved, with one of its wheels slipping off the runway. De Pinedo straightened the aircraft, only to have it veer off several more times until it was clear that he was losing control. Entirely off the tarmac, the Bellanca's momentum carried it over the grass at high speed until it plowed through a steel fence, tearing off its wings in the process. The plane tumbled for another twenty-five feet before coming to rest on its side.

De Pinedo emerged stunned and shaken and then strained to reach back into the cockpit, trying to kill the plane's engine. Within seconds, both the aircraft and its unfortunate pilot were engulfed in a blinding burst of flames.

An estimated five thousand mourners attended De Pinedo's funeral Mass at St. Patrick's Cathedral, his coffin carried to church by a horse-drawn caisson in a solemn procession led by a mounted escort of American National Guardsmen. The Italian government bore the cost of the funeral and the return of his remains back home, where he was interred with full military honors.

FEW SPECTATORS WERE ON hand when the Decennale squadron finally lifted off the water in usual sequence at dawn on July 25. As the planes reached New England near the Canadian border, Balbo transmitted messages to Mayor Kelly, Mayor O'Brien and other officials, thanking them and the citizens they represented for their generous welcome. To Roosevelt, he radioed, "Now as the Italian Atlantic Squadron approaches the boundaries of the United States, my thoughts and those of my men turn gratefully to the President of this great and noble country with such an abundance of hospitality and cordial friendship."

On July 27, the squadron flew to Shoal Harbor in Newfoundland, the launching point of the return flight over the ocean. The *Alice* and most of the other support had also docked there, their captains waiting for instructions on which zones and sectors to be patrolled. Two possible routes were delineated for the journey home, the first aiming for Ireland and an alternative one dropping southward to the Azores. Days passed waiting for constantly changing weather patterns to stabilize before it was decided that the latter path would be taken.

The support ships sailed off to their assigned sectors on the Atlantic, and the squadron finally took to the air at dawn on August 8, completing the 1,500-mile stretch from Newfoundland with little trouble after thirteen hours

The *Alice* and the submarines *Balilla* and *Millelire* docked at Newfoundland. *From* My Air Armada *(1934).*

in the air. Lieutenant Enrico Donnelli, commander of the Azores base, had earlier determined that no single harbor existed there with sufficient room to accommodate a safe landing and mooring of the entire squadron. Half of the planes, led by Pellegrini, were therefore directed to land at Horta, while Balbo's half descended at Ponta Delgada 170 miles farther east.

Now the *Atlantici* were anxious to get home and share the details of their great adventure with their families and friends. Every attempt was made to circumvent anything that might delay their departure, especially with reports of storm clouds building to the south. Shortly after the planes of the Black Group began accelerating to lift off the choppy water, one of them, Captain Ranieri's aircraft, suddenly buckled and overturned.

Rescue boats hurried to retrieve the crewmen, all badly shaken but with apparently minor injuries. Donnelli sent them to the local hospital to be checked over, and he directed the clearing of wreckage from the bay so the remainder of the flying boats could proceed on their way. Once the hospitalized men were released by the doctors, Donnelli was instructed to put them on a plane for Lisbon, the squadron's final layover point before Orbatello, where they could reunite with their comrades.

Sadly, no sooner was the squadron safely moored in Portugal than news arrived that Ranieri's copilot, Lieutenant Enrico Squalia, had gone into shock and died. The news was devastating to Balbo and every other aviator and crewman of the Decennale. All celebratory events prepared for their arrival in Lisbon were duly canceled out of respect for the expedition's latest and last tragic loss. Instead, the *Atlantici* gathered together privately in their hotel rooms to mourn their lost colleague.

None of the survivors of the wreck could shed much light on its cause. Their aircraft, they all avowed, just suddenly flipped. Ranieri was a well-seasoned pilot whose proficiency at handling his plane was beyond question. The conditions he faced at takeoff were identical to those of everyone else's, and they all were able to glide into the air without problems. There could only be speculation: one of the hulls might have struck some unseen debris in the water, or perhaps there was some structural defect that passed unnoticed during the last inspection. A conclusive reason was never determined, which further darkened an already dark episode of the enterprise when it was so close to its end.

However, none of this detracted from what had been achieved when the squadron landed on Europe's shore. In their round-trip crossing, the Italians had sent more planes over the ocean than all previous flights combined. Two lives and two aircraft had been sacrificed—a far lesser price than the twenty-three deaths and twenty-seven planes lost by other nations in the attempt to date. And again and most importantly, they had demonstrated the limitless possibilities that careful planning and organization offered for the future of intercontinental air travel.

A literal Roman triumph was waiting for Balbo and the *Atlantici* when their great venture concluded in the early evening of August 12, as their flying boats touched down on the Tyrrhenian Sea at the mouth of the Tiber River. Thousands awaited on shore to welcome the heroes home, including Mussolini, who joyfully embraced Balbo when the two men approached. A motorcade brought the airmen to Rome, the city festooned with flags and banners, glowing more vividly under massive street illuminations that overtook the failing daylight.

The principal festivities began the following morning, when the aviators, all in dress uniform, were presented to the king at the Quirinale Palace, who shook each man's hand. From there, accompanied by the Royal Air Force Band, the *Atlantici* paraded past the Coliseum, through the Arch of Constantine and finally to the Palatine Hill, all to thundering cannon blasts, batteries of fireworks and a tidal wave of cheers and applause. With imperial Roman ruins as the backdrop, and in the presence of representatives of all the armed forces, all of the government ministries and innumerable spectators, Mussolini conferred on Balbo the title of air marshal.

The formal conclusion of the Decennale took place at Orbatello the next day. King Vittorio Emanuele and his entourage arrived to review the *Atlantici*, who, again in full dress, stood at attention in the base's central piazza. After brief orations, Balbo faced the men and shouted, "In the presence and in the name of His Majesty the King, the Second Atlantic Squadron is hereby dismissed. Long live the King!"

"Long Live the king!" echoed the immediate, unanimous reply. The monarch responded with a stiff salute to the invigorating strains of *Marcia Reale* bringing the ceremony to a close. Before the men dispersed, Balbo passed down the lines, with a hand clasp, an embrace and a kiss on the cheek for each one of them.

AFTERMATH

As it turned out, Balbo's new role as air marshal would, in practice, be meaningless. Three months later, in one of his not infrequent cabinet shakeups, Mussolini announced that Balbo would be leaving the Air Ministry and assuming the role of governor general of Italy's North African colony of Libya. Balbo half-expected something like this was coming. He was all too familiar with his boss's strategy of shuffling cabinet posts and governmental offices every now and then to prevent any of the Fascist hierarchs from becoming too comfortable—or too powerful—in his position. And the newly designated air marshal fit that description on both scores.

Still, Balbo's initial reaction to the news with a mixture of anger and sadness. He truly loved his job and the *Regia Aeronautica* in particular and was no longer interested in politics. In fact, he had even developed disdain for it. For all of his rebellious nature, and though he threatened to do so in private in occasional outbursts, he couldn't bring himself to buck orders from his chief.

In January 1934, Balbo and his family duly relocated to Tripoli, and the transfer contributed to Balbo's ever-evolving relationship with Mussolini, from the start unlike that of anyone else's in the regime. The two had simultaneously risen to leadership roles in the Fascist Party's formative days, and even after Mussolini was named the prime minister of the kingdom, Balbo's behavior toward him was more as an old comrade in arms than that of an underling. He always used informal pronouns when addressing his boss and never hesitated to bluntly speak his mind.

Balbo was forced to continually downplay the widely circulated assumption, particularly in the foreign press, that he was Mussolini's undoubted heir apparent, the only man in the Kingdom of Italy who could, and someday almost certainly would, fill Il Duce's shoes. Despite his emphatic dismissals of the thought, it was pretty much a given, one that Mussolini himself privately acknowledged. That, of course, was the reason Balbo was dismissed from the Air Ministry and sent off to virtual exile in Libya in the first place. The prosaic job of administering Italy's North African colony was a way of getting his name out of the foreign press, which had come to treat him like an A-list celebrity. Such popularity, Mussolini worried, emboldened an already independent-minded potential rival and rendered him immune to constraint.

As a pacification move, Mussolini avoided interference in the way Balbo governed Libya, allowing it to develop almost like the former air minister's own private island. In exchange, Balbo was expected to distance himself from the kingdom's internal business, returning to Italy only for an occasional conference or similar state function. Although Balbo was not happy to leave the air ministry, the new arrangement was a mutually welcomed departure from their past relationship and possibly the only viable solution to a situation in which two unusually strong-willed men find themselves in the same room.

Mussolini, for instance, tried to micromanage the Decennale cruise, continuously messaging Balbo with unsolicited suggestions and advice each step of the way until the much-annoyed air minister had to ask him to back off. For Mussolini, it was an unnecessary reminder that Balbo was not just another one of the sycophants who only told him what he wanted to hear. Despite the intent to sideline him, Balbo's tendency to dismiss or undermine those policies of the regime he found unreasonable only intensified as the decade progressed.

Balbo and other notables of the Fascist *gerarchia*, the old guard who led the party from its earliest days, were growing uncomfortable with the direction in which the regime was heading by the late 1930s. But Balbo aside, their opinions were expressed only in private letters or diaries. Balbo had the nerve to repeatedly say so out loud and outside closed doors. By then, Mussolini was drawing closer to Hitler, despite having brushed off the Nazi leader as a buffoonish lunatic only a few years earlier. The fear was that the developing military alliance between the Fascists and Nazis would evolve into a moral alliance, as well as an endorsement of Germany's racial and antisemitic doctrines, which the majority of Italians found repulsive. When their fears came true with the regime's enactment of the 1938 antisemitic laws, Balbo sharply rebuked Mussolini for "licking Germany's boots."

His contempt toward this shameful course manifested in other ways. On occasion, Balbo was obligated to host diplomatic visits to Tripoli by high Nazi officials, something he very much disliked doing. On one such occasion, he gave a dinner for Hermann Goering, making sure to also invite a half dozen prominent Libyan Jews. A visit to a local synagogue was included in the German's tour of the city, and as a departure gift, he was given a reproduction of a Roman statuette crafted by a Jewish artisan. When Germany invaded Poland, Balbo flew straightway to Rome in a useless attempt to convince Mussolini that Hitler's unprovoked aggression and its accompanying Nazi-Soviet pact were grounds for a renunciation of the Axis. Italy, he warned repeatedly, was being inexorably pulled in a direction that could only bring the nation and the Fascist Party to an ignominious end.

The pro-German Fascist hierarch Roberto Farinacci, who did little to hide his own personal hatred of Balbo, repeatedly disparaged him to Mussolini as an annoying and even dangerous obstructionist who found fault with every decision or policy that came out of Rome, whether it was the war against Ethiopia, intervention in the Spanish civil war or the alienation of Italy's traditional allies. But when war was finally declared against Great Britain and France in the spring of 1940, Balbo simply resigned himself to do his duty and, with the meager resources he was provided, took up arms in what he knew was a hopeless cause. Fate, however, stepped in to relieve him from that dreaded task.

On June 28, 1940, a mere two weeks after Italy had entered World War II, Balbo's aircraft was blasted out of the sky by anti aircraft guns near the Libyan town of Tobruk. On board with him were eight others, among them the journalist Quilici and his nephew Lino—all instantly obliterated. The shocking news circulated the world at lightning speed, with Italian newspapers spinning Balbo's demise as the result of a heroic aerial clash with the enemy. In truth, though, nobody to this day knows with absolute certainty why Balbo and his companions had taken to the sky that day or where they were planning on going.

The fact that the shells that assaulted him came not from British but from Italian guns rapidly triggered more questions and speculations. The gun crew claimed that they had mistaken Balbo's plane as a straggler in the British air raid that had earlier occurred. But the aircraft, a Savoia Marchetti SM-79, had a distinct profile, its tri-motor design unlike anything in Britain's aerial arsenal, and the letters I-MANU painted in large bold letters on the undersides of both wings (in honor of Balbo's wife, Emanuella) should have been easily distinguishable through any basic pair of binoculars.

The inquiry that followed was swift and cursory. A revelation that an incompetent artillery crew had killed a living legend like Balbo was hardly a wartime morale booster for the Italian public. Inevitably, some began to wonder if Balbo's plane had been purposefully targeted. Balbo's wife, for one, was absolutely convinced of that. This suspicion was unnecessarily fueled by Galeazzo Ciano, Mussolini's son-in-law, who carelessly quipped at a cocktail party that Balbo's demise was, perhaps, not an accident at all. His opposition to the war, and particularly to waging it alongside the Germans, was common knowledge. With friends and relatives on board, was he intending to jump over to the British side? The latter thought was instantly rejected by everyone who knew him or anything significant about him. Ever a loyal disciple of Mazzini, he was too much a patriot to ever abandon his post in defending Italy from any wartime enemy. Although the debate over the causes of the incident has never been truly settled, the general consensus is that Balbo was on his way to inspect Italian ground forces and had been simply shot down by friendly fire.

After a suitable mourning was allowed to pass, the official word from Rome to both the Italian press and the government hierarchy was blunt. Balbo is dead, and there must be no more mention of him. The British, however, were not constrained by such decrees. Shortly after the incident, they sent an aircraft over the Italian lines from which a box of flowers was dropped along with a note from the commander in chief of the British Royal Air Force in that wartime theater; it read, "The British Royal Air Force expresses its sympathy in the death of General Balbo, a great leader and gallant aviator, personally known to me, whom fate has placed on the opposite side."

AN OVERVIEW OF THE AIR CRUISE LEGACY

As one of the most memorable events of the world's fair, and certainly of the whole year, the Decennale air cruise captured the attention of millions across the globe. What contributed to the advancement of aviation, however, has since been questioned and debated. In fact, few aeronautical feats have spawned such a widely divergent range of appraisal. In 1933, of course, it was universally acclaimed as a giant step toward the eventual realization of regular, intercontinental air travel. Yet later commentators, especially those viewing the topic from a political perspective, have summarily dismissed it as a shallow publicity stunt in which the primary objective had as much to do with satisfying the outsized ego of a glory-craving regime than it did with practical achievement. They support this view by noting that the Italians took no follow-up action to broaden the path that they had supposedly opened. Once their hunger for acclaim had been sated, their interest in bridging the hemispheres by air seems to have dropped cold.

However, unfailingly passing unnoticed are the discernible parallels between this rather harsh assessment and NASA's own Apollo space program of the 1960s. With America's overriding ambition to beat the Russians to the moon as its admitted motivation, this enterprise was also "dropped cold" not long after that feat was accomplished. In both cases, high costs also adversely affected the willingness for further pursuit. To Italy's critics, of course, this only indicates that the kingdom and its Fascist government were

Poster by Umberto Di Lazzaro. *Author's collection.*

merely mimicking the role of Great Power—one that they had no business playing—although such remarks could never logically be directed against the United States.

There can be no denying that the 1933 cruise was intended to score high points for Italian prestige. This it did, and although later day critics generally attribute much of the applause to the mood of the times in which a disillusioned, economically devastated world looked desperately for reassurance of a better future, it's both inaccurate and unfair to dismiss the enterprise as a flashy Fascist sideshow.

As noted earlier, any ocean flight still deserved front-page coverage in 1933. The Italian effort, however, was distinguished not only by its unprecedented number of participants but also by how it signaled the arrival of an important turning point in aeronautical development. Tightly controlled conditions and ground support networks would henceforth play a bigger role than the individual initiative and reckless derring-do that had characterized aviation's pioneering years. Yet attempts at deprecation are made even with this, as some argue that compared to the speedier and more direct flights of other aviators, the complicated, slow-moving apparatus set up by Balbo and his staff foreshadowed modern intercontinental air travel in only the dimmest way.

Here Balbo would be the first to agree. In the midst of the euphoria and applause surrounding the cruise, it was the Italian air minister himself who reminded everyone that he and his collaborators had only created a template to be enhanced and refined before routine transoceanic aerial traffic would become a reality. Could he respond to his latter-day critics, he would again stress that the avoidance of needless risk characterized the enterprise—surely the sane way to proceed if the opening of commercial air lanes between the hemispheres was indeed the ultimate goal. That viewpoint was recognized time after time in the countless speeches, magazine articles and newspaper editorials generated by the event. Unfailingly found somewhere in each narrative were words like *science*, *technology*, *precision*, *preparation* and, above all, *safety*.

The tragic fact that part of the Decennale's cost included the loss of two young lives did nothing to diminish its often-reiterated objective of minimizing risk. The sometimes lengthy holdups at various landing stations on both the outbound and inbound stages were invariably due to unfavorable weather, quite often the very conditions that wouldn't have stopped someone like Wiley Post or even De Pinedo during their own aerial tours. Even today's incalculably superior equipment, communications and surface support have been unable to fully eliminate aeronautical fatalities. In 1933, plane crashes and deaths were still expected almost as a matter of course. That Balbo had left Italy with twenty-five planes and returned with twenty-three after two ocean crossings was a meritorious feat.

It's impossible to fully assess the impact made by the flight without including the favorable impression made on the American public by the air minister himself. On the most superficial level, he undeniably projected a dashing, romantic appeal. It was, after all, a much more romantic era, one deeply infused with Hollywood-inspired glamor. Many of those who met him in person, women in particular, or even those who simply fawned over his pictures in daily rotogravures detected, or more

Camera ad. *Author's collection.*

accurately imagined, a note of exotic roguishness belied by his spotless, crisp military tunic, erect posture and impeccably correct social skills. Well polished yet approachable and affable, he displayed respectful deference to others and formed friendships with natural ease. Mayor Kelly spoke for thousands when he declared that Balbo "had stolen the heart of Chicago by his courage and personality."

This was by no means overlooked by the city's business community, which instinctively sought to capitalize on it wherever possible. One leading department store advertised a new line of women's hats designed to resemble Balbo's old wartime Alpine headgear, promising customers the "same swagger and daring attitude" of the Italian air chief. Whether selling spark plugs, cameras or near beer, manufacturers and retailers ran display ads linking their products with the Decennale cruise. Souvenirs proliferated, and vendors inside and outside the fair hawked miniature Italian flags and portraits of Balbo printed on embossed, frameable cardboard down to two-inch lapel buttons. A trading card company even included him in its series of great aviators.

The cudgel-wielding squadrista leader of ten years earlier was nowhere to be seen. But there was no doubt that he had once existed. Certainly the mayors, commissioners and governors, even up to the president of the

Hat ad. *Author's collection.*

United States, were quite aware of that, but in no way did this impede the admiration and even affection for Balbo that they all very publicly expressed. Nor was the entire U.S. Congress deluded when it voted without dissension to award the Italian air minister with the Distinguished Flying Cross. Nor did Cardinal Mundelein and the pope himself exhibit any visible reluctance in extending cordial salutations to a man once accused of complicity of the murder of a Catholic priest.

Balbo represented a government that came to power through revolution and violence. Plenty of governments had come to power through revolution and with a far greater degree of violence, some surely rationalized, and had been eventually accepted as legitimate members of the global community.

Communism and anarchy, insidiously dangerous to the most basic American principles, were in fundamental opposition to the Fascist regime, and this, too, softened much of the stark differences between the political structures of Fascist Italy and the United States. Except for the briefest of episodes in the 1890s, the relations between the two nations had remained friendly.

Americans, like the rest of the world, were not sure what to make of Mussolini and the Fascist Party as they began their rise to power. But within a few years, a stable, functional nation was emerging from the economic and social chaos that plagued it in the immediate postwar years. The regime, outsiders reasoned, must be doing something right. World leaders, even those proponents of sharply divergent ideologies like Winston Churchill and Mahatma Gandhi, were referring to it or its leader in positive fashion.

Gasoline ad. *From the* Aero Digest, *August 1932.*

Standard Oil ad. *Author's collection.*

The word *fascist*, certainly in more recent years, is overused as a synonym for "Nazi." And indeed, Adolf Hitler was seizing control of Germany during the very same year Balbo led the Decennale to Chicago. But no one would have confused the two political movements back then. The antisemitism and race-based doctrines of the Nazis were repugnant to millions outside Germany, even in that far less tolerant age, and Italian Fascism, too, renounced those concepts, although Mussolini would later embrace them after the creation of the Axis.

Blood flowed truly enough in Italy during the political turmoil of postwar years, with corpses sometimes left behind in the aftermath. Occasional deadly assaults, like the Minzoni incident and the equally shocking murder by overzealous Fascist thugs of the Socialist leader Giacomo Matteotti, were a matter of record. But for all of this brutality, there never occurred anything remotely similar to a Night of the Long Knives or a *Kristallnacht* or Dachau. Even during his visit to the Soviet Union, Balbo's hosts asked how the word *revolution* could justifiably be applied to Fascism's ascent since relatively few lives had been lost in the process compared to the blood-soaked events in Russia beginning in 1917.

Capital punishment, outlawed by King Umberto I in 1889, was reinstated under the Fascists, but it was rarely imposed. Less than a dozen criminal trials ended with a death sentence between 1926 and 1940, the same period during which the United States was averaging 150 executions per year and the Soviet and Nazi courts were routinely condemning numbers deep in the thousands.

This, of course, is not an exoneration or apology for Mussolini's Fascist regime. It was repressive, authoritarian, restrictive and totally incompatible with the rights and freedoms under which Americans were fortunate to live. The differences are especially severe for the vicious, Nazi-controlled version of Italian Fascism that emerged in Central and Northern Italy after 1943. But again, this was the early 1930s. Italy was not the United States. It had a radically different and far more ancient and complicated past and faced a radically different set of challenges and obstacles. Whether Fascism was the political structure the Italians needed to work through their problems was theirs to decide. Although no rational observer would ever describe it as benign, Italian Fascism in 1933 didn't conjure the images of unbridled brutality associated with it today.

Not for a single moment, too, were the populations of Chicago, New York or anywhere else the squadron landed left unaware of Fascism's role in its success. Balbo was careful to never omit an obligatory statement of praise or attribution to Mussolini for instilling Italians with the discipline and spirit that made achievements like the Decennale possible. The *saluto romano*, right arm thrust out and upward, was given continuously and almost everywhere. Fascist imagery typically adorned, often overpoweringly, the various venues at which the *Atlantici* appeared. The Italian pavilion, the epicenter of Balbo's presence at the world's fair, was a virtual Fascist temple. With the notable exclusion of the radical leftists who, while he was in town, staged demonstrations and handed out leaflets denouncing Balbo and Fascism, no one else appeared to be bothered by it. In the midst of the euphoria generated by Balbo's arrival, the *Chicago Examiner* was only one of many American voices hailing the regime's achievements, declaring that its doctrines were "swiftly transforming an ancient people into a homogeneous nation more American than the United States."

Italian Americans, to no one's surprise, idolized Balbo. Professor Dominic Candeloro, curator of the Italian Cultural Center in Stone Park, Illinois, a historian and author recognized as the leading authority on Chicago's Italian Americans, described the arrival of the *Atlantici* as unquestionably the greatest day in that community's history. Like the impressions projected by the Fair's Italian Village being in such stark contradiction to that of the Italian pavilion, the American public generally maintained contrasting impressions of Italian culture. There was the image of supreme sophistication, exemplified by the flawlessly tailored and white-gloved Prince Potenziani, over whom the North Shore socialites competed to be seated next to at an afternoon tea, or perhaps even host a dinner for in their own elegant mansions. There were the performers and directors of the Civic Opera, purveyors of the finest of the fine arts. And there were the passionate Latin lovers, as classically embodied by Rudolph Valentino on the movie screen.

That was one side. Another was the image to which Balbo himself had alluded at Madison Square Garden: the lowly, semi-literate immigrant; objects of ridicule; organ grinders; excitable, gesticulating fruit vendors; gardeners and ditch diggers—all butchering the English language as they comically fumbled their way through life in the New World. On the other, more sinister hand were the criminals, swarthy thugs who were corrupting the nation through vice and illicit activities of organized crime. Plenty of notorious Irish and Jewish gangsters plied their illicit business on Chicago streets with no less blood-soaked diligence, but the yoke of notoriety was placed on the Italians. In 1931, Warner Bros. released *Little Caesar*, with Edward G. Robinson playing the vulgar and uncouth mobster Enrico Bandello. From this seminal film emerged the stereotype of the brutish and evil Italian American mafioso that continues unhindered to this day, long after all other ethnic and racial stereotypes have been condemned and banished by the media and academia for being, at the very least, in bad taste.

It was the latter brand of defamatory imagery that adhered most inextricably to the Italian Americans in the public's mind. And with this, it's not too difficult to understand the redeeming explosion of pride that coursed through their community, flushing away like some marvelous elixir the sense of inferiority and degradation imposed on it from every direction.

To watch a judge, a police detective or any other figure of authority who, just days earlier, had perhaps belittled or intimidated them now respectfully take off his hat to the Italian aviator had no short lasting effect. Italian American fraternal groups renamed their lodges after him, and businesses likewise altered their names in homage to their beloved hero.

Until the squadron's arrival, Italians in America had clung tightly to Columbus as the best argument for their right to be in this country when they were scorned as undesirable stock by the Anglo-Saxon and Scots-Irish majority. But Balbo, no distant figure of the distant past, was a living, breathing hero of the present, and the level of esteem to which he was elevated, if momentarily, eclipsed that of the great admiral of the ocean sea.

The impression left on Balbo by the United States was no less impactful and enduring, the supreme confirmation of the economic and industrial muscle he had observed on his first trip here in 1929. Even under the stress of the Great Depression, it had no equal in the world. He couldn't conceive how any other nation might be foolish enough to engage America in war, a conviction he would much later express when Mussolini pulled their unwilling country closer to the impending global conflict.

On a personal level, Balbo genuinely liked Americans. Their down-to-earth, egalitarian nature appealed to his lifelong attraction to republicanism. But more than anything else, he admired their boundless energy, the irrepressibly high spirit and self-confidence of the citizens of what was still, compared to old Europe, a young and vibrant nation. And, of course, he had made many friends here, some with whom he would continue to keep in touch over the ensuing years.

Had he survived another seven months to witness it, Balbo's adverse reaction to his country's going to war against the United States can well be imagined. From a practical standpoint, he knew that Italy was not prepared to effectively fight Great Britain, let alone the greatest industrial power in all of human history. He had been there twice, he often reminded Mussolini, and anyone who had seen the actual breadth and depth of American wealth and industrial power would conclude that here was a nation never to be challenged. It's difficult to envision Balbo not being among the Fascist leaders who finally conspired to force Mussolini's resignation as the war grew increasingly catastrophic. In fact, he most likely would have acted sooner.

CHICAGO'S CIVIC TRIBUTES

On April 5, 1962, an Alitalia DC-8 touched down at Chicago's new O'Hare International Airport, completing an eleven-hour nonstop flight from Rome. Among its passengers were twelve older gentlemen, their high military ranks belied by civilian business suits. Only small, winged lapel pins hinted to their identities. The men, all balding or graying, formed a group representing the surviving crew members of the Italian aerial voyage to the Century of Progress World's Fair. Many of their eighty-four former comrades had perished in the world war that rumbled across Europe less than a decade after their sensational flight. But that day, the twelve, most of them now generals in the Italian air force, had come as Chicago's guests to celebrate the commencement of regular air service to the city by Italy's national airline.

Limousines were soon gliding down the Kennedy Expressway, itself barely two years old, bringing the aging *Atlantici* to city hall, where they were surprised to find U.S. Air Force, Army, Navy and Marine Corps color guards, all standing at attention and presenting arms, surrounded by some two thousand applauding civilian onlookers. The richly fluid and melodic strains of traditional Italian-style symphonic marches, rendered by a military band, echoed against the towering buildings along LaSalle Street.

Mayor Richard J. Daley led the welcoming party, extending warmest greetings upon the veteran airmen's return to Chicago twenty-nine years after their first historic visit. And indeed, the twelve men must have experienced a powerful sense of déjà vu, as Daley's speech was followed by a week of banquets, tours and receptions. Immediately after the welcoming ceremony, during which the mayor bestowed honorary Chicago citizenship to his guests, the party headed for a luncheon at the nearby Sherman House Hotel. There they were met by Illinois governor Otto Kerner, who, like Daley and most of their hosts, recalled his own memories of the awe and excitement that electrified Chicago when the Italian aviators, so young and heroic back then, touched down on Lake Michigan in 1933.

Here and at subsequent events, the inevitable comparisons were made between the state of aeronautics in the 1930s and the 1960s, and recognition of valor and skill was lavished on the Italian aviators for surmounting the many of the then daunting challenges of transoceanic air travel that had since become routine. The twelve men, for their part, responded to the continuous declamations of praise with the unpretentious discretion they had learned as cadets in Balbo's academy so long ago. Deeply touched by the kindness and consideration of their hosts, they voiced assurances that this current visit had only strengthened the special affection they held for the city that had given them so many pleasant memories.

In the remaining days of their visit, the Italians were taken to the site of the former fair in Burnham Park. Here they saw the Balbo Monument standing in the shadow of Soldier Field, where they were once wildly cheered by so many thousands of Chicagoans. Another luncheon was held at the Museum of Science and Industry, a surviving structure from the 1893 Columbian Exposition World's Fair in Jackson Park on Chicago's South Side. There they were presented with photos and regalia recalling their visit to the city's second world's fair, among which was a scale model of an SM-55X, which they carefully examined in a mixture of humorous delight and nostalgic sentimentality.

But the most revealing demonstration of the bond between the aviators and Chicago was witnessed at a banquet at the Blackstone Hotel hosted by General and Mrs. Julius Klein on the evening preceding their return trip home. Born in Chicago of Jewish immigrant parents, Klein was an Illinois National Guardsman serving as aide to the 33rd Division's commander, Lieutenant General Roy Keehn, at the time of the Italian air squadron's arrival in Chicago. Illinois governor Henry Horner had placed Keehn in charge of security during Balbo's visit, and he, in turn, assigned Klein to personally accompany and attend to the needs of the Italian air minister and his retinue. Over the next few days, so cordial a friendship developed between Klein and Captain Giuseppe Teucci, one of Balbo's officers, that the two men maintained occasional correspondence with each other long after the Italian squadron's departure.

While Klein was still a youth, his family temporarily repatriated to Moravia but later returned to the United States. His sister Fannie, however, opted to remain in Europe, marrying Nathan Ticho, an industrialist and prominent local Jewish community leader. The couple eventually had four sons, only to see their prosperous and happy family life abruptly shattered when Nazi Germany annexed Czechoslovakia in 1938. With his clothing factory confiscated by the Gestapo, Nathan and his brother were arrested and imprisoned in the Dachau concentration camp.

Klein, now a U.S. Army colonel, was alerted of these events in a letter from Fannie, whose American citizenship protected her from her own arrest. She implored her brother to find a way of rescuing the family from its plight. But recourse was almost nonexistent. Although the United States was not yet at war with the Germans, diplomatic relations were strained, and it was American policy to avoid intervention in Germany's internal affairs. There seemed to be no route to any Nazi official who might be persuaded to intercede on the Ticho family's behalf. Then Klein remembered Balbo and Teucci. Both men were still connected to the Italian government, after all, and the newly signed Pact of Steel had bound Italy and Germany as close political and military allies. It was certainly worth a try.

In May 1940, Klein called on Cook County Superior Court judge John A. Sbarbaro, an old friend and one of the local officials who had welcomed the *Atlantici* to Chicago seven years earlier. The judge, who maintained contacts within the Italian government, translated and promptly dispatched Klein's appeal to Balbo himself.

By this time, of course, Balbo as governor of Libya had been virtually severed from developments in Europe. Though with genuine sympathy, he stated as much in responding to Klein's appeal, pointing out that he and Marshal Hermann Goering, the sole high German official with whom he had any significant acquaintance, were not well-disposed toward each other, and a favorable outcome would be unlikely. However, he promised to pass the matter on to the air attaché at the Italian embassy in Berlin, who happened to be none other than Giuseppe Teucci, to see what he could do.

The succession of events that followed are not entirely clear, but according to Nathan's son Charles, who, decades later, retold the story for the *Jerusalem Post*, the matter eventually made its way to the desk of Benito Mussolini himself. Whatever direction the course had taken, in a short amount of time Nathan Ticho was released from Dachau and reunited with his family. All were given documents of clearance to depart unhindered for the United States.

Captain Teucci. *From* Official Book of the Flight of Gen. Italo Balbo *(1933).*

After Italy surrendered to the Allies in 1943, Teucci, in a curious twist of fate, was himself imprisoned in the Sachsenhausen concentration camp for refusing to switch allegiance to the Italian Social Republic, the Nazi puppet state set up in the German-controlled portions of the Kingdom of Italy. Transferred to a prison camp there, he and several other high-ranking officers made a daring escape and spent the rest of the war years fighting alongside the Partisans against the Nazi occupiers.

Klein assured his banquet guests that his family's profound gratitude and affection toward Teucci and Balbo had never diminished and expressed the regret that the latter had lost his own life before the matter came to its happy resolution. The first return of at least some of the *Atlantici* to Chicago ended on that moving note.

Eleven years later, through the efforts of Chicago's Joint Civic Committee of Italian Americans, more than twice as many of Balbo's former crewmen were flown back to mark the fortieth anniversary of their historic aerial ocean crossing and to join in the city's 1973 Columbus Day festivities. The twenty-seven veteran airmen were the highlight of the annual parade and later again welcomed at the Museum of Science and Industry to attend a seminar and special exhibit on Italy's contributions to aeronautics. Joining them on behalf of his father was Paolo Balbo, now a successful attorney and author, as well as Countess Maria Caproni, daughter of the great airplane builder and director of the Caproni Aeronautical Museum in Vizzola Ticino. The schedule of events concluded, as usual, with a banquet, this time at Chicago's LaSalle Hotel.

Only five surviving *Atlantici* were able to attend the fiftieth anniversary commemoration of the flight, again fused into Chicago's Columbus Day activities. By this time, the number of those who had firsthand memories of Balbo's arrival was thinning significantly. The press coverage of the two earlier visits, largely by reporters and editors whose fond and nostalgic recollections of the actual event was clearly in evidence, was giving way to younger journalists who had no personal connection to it. The friendly, even affectionate character of such newspaper stories and commentaries was replaced by detachment and even hostility.

Chicago Sun Times columnist Vernon Jarrett urged the Museum of Science and Industry, again serving as the venue for an Italian aeronautical exhibit, to divorce itself from participation. By allowing Balbo's 1933 flight, which he breezily dismissed as a cheap "stunt," to be showcased within its walls, the institution's involvement was tantamount to an endorsement of fascism. Jarrett went on to remind his readers that Balbo's air force had mercilessly obliterated Ethiopians in East Africa, despite the fact that the *Regia Aeronautica* had been out of his hands for two years when that conflict began.

Still, that flawed observation took hold in the mind of Chicago alderwoman Helen Shiller, who in 1990 proposed changing the name of Balbo Drive to Nelson Mandela Drive. The act, according to Shiller, would be a grand rendering of poetic justice against the bloodthirsty fascist who died while dropping bombs on Africans. During this author's subsequent conversation with Shiller, it was learned that the research on which her pronouncement was based did not extend beyond sending her son to look up Balbo's name in a public library encyclopedia.

Shiller was hardly the first to propose the renaming of Balbo Drive. Two years before he penned his objections to the 1983 commemoration and while lobbying for the city to pay tribute to Jean Baptiste Pointe du Sable, Vernon Jarrett zeroed in on Balbo Drive as a vulnerable target. The action, he argued, would serve the double purpose of purging the city of an embarrassing fascist relic and fulfilling long-overdue recognition of the African-Haitian Du Sable, accepted as the first non-indigenous settler in the Chicago area.

Opposition to Balbo's name on a Chicago street sign was present from the very moment it appeared on the map. But until the 1940s, it appeared exclusively in the newspapers and journals of the far left. Only a few weeks after a state of war was declared between Italy and the United States, Chicago Fifth Ward alderman (and later Illinois senator) Paul H. Douglas suggested that the street be renamed after Giuseppe Garibaldi, the universally respected and beloved nineteenth-century freedom fighter. The proposal didn't get far. Balbo had already perished before the two countries had become enemies, others argued, and the sketchy circumstances surrounding his death left open the possibility that he personally remained a friend to America to the hour of his premature demise. Another alderman insisted that the city council postpone any street name changes until the truth behind Balbo's death was ascertained. With the city and the nation in the process of massive mobilization, the proposition was hardly a priority, and it was speedily dropped.

It wasn't until 1946 that the first serious movement to remove Balbo's name from the city atlas began in earnest. With war-inspired patriotism still at fever pitch, a coalition of Chicago politicians, businessmen, veteran groups and academic organizations proposed changing the street name to honor Lieutenant Commander John Charles Waldron, a heroic U.S. Navy pilot and squadron leader who died at the Battle of Midway. Though certainly deserving of memorializing, Waldron, who was born in South Dakota and raised in Canada, had no connections to Chicago, and why he in particular was chosen over any number of war heroes rooted closer to home is unclear. In truth, it's likely that the name of any distinguished American war hero would have served the coalition's primary purpose, which was to cleanse Chicago of any prewar connections to Italian Fascism.

From the moment he was presented with it, the idea was opposed by Mayor Edward Kelly, the same Mayor Kelly who had proudly handed Balbo the Key to the City in 1933. A master Chicago politician, he skillfully utilized every tactic and maneuver to delay and block the resolution from coming to vote. While some of this may well be attributed to his personal admiration toward Balbo, at least as much was fear of alienating the city's Italian American voting bloc. The sentiment was shared by dozens of aldermen, and it speaks to the unique status that Balbo's name held in the Italian American community.

Even though they were fighting their ancestral homeland, no ethnic group in the United States surpassed the Italian Americans in patriotism. They made up a full 10 percent of the U.S. armed forces, with their numbers reaching over 1 million men and women in uniform, fourteen of whom were Medal of Honor recipients. No honest person in their right mind could question their loyalty to America. Yet the jolt of pride infused in them by the 1933 flight remained powerful enough to force politicians like Kelly to duck and dodge their way through the street name controversy.

But other politicians and community leaders of Italian descent endorsed the name change, advocating for that cause with an exuberance that occasionally led to some recklessly inaccurate public statements. Mr. Ruben Cinquini, president of the Chicago chapter of the Mazzini Society, provided a painful example with the observation that Italian Americans "lacking all the facts are inclined favorably to Balbo." Yet, Cinquini immediately followed up with his own blatantly fact-free remark in an attempt to strip Balbo even of any merit from a technological sense, declaring preposterously in the *Chicago Tribune*, "Although many look on Balbo as a great flyer, the fact is he didn't know the first thing about flying a plane."

Like others, Cinquini's assessment that support for the retention of Balbo Drive was based on ignorance only revealed his own misunderstanding of the situation, and one shared by all proponents of changing the street name. Whether motivated by the desire to honor Waldron or simply to scrub Italo Balbo from the city's memory, advocates for the change suggested placating Italian American voters by either placing the name of another famous but less controversial Italian over the former 7th Street or on the sign of some other city road.

A compromise of sorts was reached in 1948, when the city council approved the rededication of a short stretch of 16th Street near Soldier Field in Waldron's honor, just yards, incidentally, from the Roman column. Of course, this didn't satisfy those whose main objective from the onset was to cancel Balbo's memorialization, but the proposal to pay civic homage to Waldron had gained such popular momentum on its own that where it would happen actually became a side issue.

Around that same time, another call for the removal of Chicago's tributes to Balbo came not from local activists but from Italy's post–World War II government. By coincidence, while the Balbo-Waldron debate was still in high gear, Italian prime minister Alcide De Gasperi happened to be visiting Chicago as part of an American tour seeking reconstruction loans for his war-battered nation. Asked for an opinion on the street name business, his aides brushed off inquiring reporters that how Chicago handled the issue was none of Italy's business.

However, Alberto Tarchiani, Italy's first postwar ambassador to the United States, stated that the reopening of diplomatic relations between the two nations was, at a very minimum, awkward with monuments to the Fascist era still standing in a major American city. His suggestion that they be discarded was tossed aside by the newly elected Chicago Mayor Martin Kennelly, who regarded the tributes not as political statements but solely as commemorations to the city's role in a great technological achievement. This point of view was tersely summed up in his reported reply to the proposal: "Why? Didn't Balbo fly across the ocean?" Ironically, with the debate still unsettled seventy years later, some anti-Balbo activists suggested Kennelly's name as a possible replacement on the street sign. That, at least, had a greater probability than another proposal some years later to change the name to honor Chicago clothier Morris B. Sachs,

At the approach of the Decennale's fiftieth anniversary, Northwestern University professor J. Fred MacDonald issued a new demand for a street name change in a *Chicago Tribune* commentary. In it, he placed Balbo in the same despicable category as Hitler and Himmler and scornfully dismissed the historic two-way transatlantic crossing that had taken years to meticulously plan as a "public relations stunt." The professor expressed his inability to comprehend why Chicagoans had made such a big deal over it.

The unabashed references to Fascism and Mussolini all over its base render the Roman column the least subtle of the three tributes. The two-thousand-year-old pillar was unveiled in 1934 in front of the Italian pavilion and still stands at that original site. Sent as a gift from the Fascist government as a token of gratitude for the mammoth welcome Chicago had extended to the *Atlantici*, it originally stood at the ancient Roman port of Ostia not far from the point where the Decennale concluded and is the oldest antiquity in the Chicago Park District's inventory.

The column's ceremonious unveiling, a year to the day after the squadron's landing on Lake Michigan, was led by Mayor Kelly and Major Landis and was highlighted by a speech by Balbo himself, broadcast over the NBC and RCA networks, in which he again expressed his gratitude to Chicago and America. "Let this column stand as a symbol of increasing friendship between the people of Italy," he concluded. The Chicago Park District and city council concurred, and when the fair's structures and attractions were dismantled, the Roman column remained exactly where it was first unveiled.

While the more visible Balbo Drive has historically drawn the most objections, the column continues to have its share. In 1993, local Puerto Rican activists—infuriated over the Chicago Park District's refusal to erect a statue of Pedro Albizu Campos, a militant proponent of Puerto Rican independence suspected of plotting the assassination of President Truman—issued a public condemnation of the city's supposed hypocrisy by permitting the Roman column to remain in place at taxpayer's expense. That latter point didn't strike much of a note, since the costs to maintain the much-neglected antiquity never extended further than mowing the lawn around it. The city held firm and rejected the argument.

The 1996 reconfiguration of DuSable Lake Shore Drive sequestered the column away in a lonely, hard-to-reach spot near the lake, but this didn't hide it from controversy. In recent years, a national reexamination of the appropriateness of thousands of tributes, statues and commemorations honoring historical individuals whose lives and deeds don't conform, in whole or in part, to modern standards and sensibilities inevitably caught up to the column. Answer Chicago, a social justice coalition, staged a protest demonstration in 2017, during which one of its organizers creatively associated it with racism and a rise in white supremacy. That curious point of view was echoed by Fourth Ward alderman Sophia King, who remarked to the *Chicago Reader* that "Balbo is a symbol of racial and ethnic supremacy."

In any case, decades of acid rain, deferred maintenance and utter neglect have taken their toll on the already ancient column, and it continues to steadily deteriorate. Its ultimate disposition may well be determined by the weathering forces of time, with the elements gnawing away until public safety concerns require its removal.

Even in such an event, the deconstruction of the monument won't be easy or cheap. The oldest and most priceless artifact in the Chicago Park District's custody, it would have to be handled under the careful supervision of archaeologists and structural specialists, in addition to taking extraordinarily delicate transportation measures.

The civic tribute least associated with Balbo, the Columbus Monument, at Roosevelt Road and Columbus Drive, suffered the harshest fate, being the target of such vicious abuse and vandalism in the wake of the 2020 George Floyd incident that police were placed on site to prevent its literal destruction. Mayor Lori Lightfoot ordered the fifteen-foot bronze image of Columbus covered with a tarp and finally removed, ostensibly to protect it from further damage.

The monument's component concerning Balbo is a barely noticeable commemorative engraving on the statue's massive octagonal base that reads, "This Monument has seen the Glory of the Wings of Italy led by Italo Balbo—July 15, 1933." So obscure has this tribute remained over the

decades that even those who have actively demanded the obliteration of Balbo's name from the Chicago landscape have always overlooked it. Not until the base was attacked by the overzealous, spray paint–wielding mob did his detractors discover this additional object of their outrage.

The opposition directed against the other monuments has not yet approached the intensity and physical abuse suffered by the Columbus monument. But in recent years it persists to a degree that surpasses even that of the objections aimed at Balbo Drive in the immediate post–World War II era. The *Chicago Tribune*, the same newspaper that had lavished unbounded

Columbus statue. *Author's collection.*

accolades on Balbo in 1933, endorsed a petition drawn up by seven professors from Northwestern, Loyola and Chicago universities in 2011, yet again demanding the removal of the Balbo tributes. The misinformation and flawed suppositions used to make their case were so frequent that they could be explained only by intentional deception or simply sloppy research.

The petition claimed that, as governor of Libya, Balbo "supervised concentration camps in which thousands of civilians perished." This charge was obviously meant to conjure the image of Balbo as a sort of Italian Adolf Eichmann, a demonic, genocidal criminal. Concentration camps had indeed been set up in Libya by the coldhearted and intolerant General Rodolfo Graziani during the colonial pacification period prior to Balbo's administration. When Balbo became governor in 1934, he closed these camps and released the internees. By contemporary standards, Balbo's administration of Libya was regarded favorably both in its progressive policies in the treatment of the native population and through the construction and provision of hospitals, schools, roads and a long list of other infrastructural improvements. It was his stated intent to grant full Italian citizenship to all of Libya's inhabitants, regardless of race, a measure that was thwarted by Mussolini's half-hearted imitation of Nazi racial policies. Only after his death, and especially as German forces assumed control of the fighting in North Africa, did the camps reappear.

The petition further asserted that "in Italy itself, in which Italo Balbo's crimes are well known, no streets are named after him," inadvertently revealing either more shoddy research on the part of the academic authors or a deliberate falsehood. In truth, there's a street named *Via Italo Balbo* in at least twenty Italian municipalities across the peninsula and the Island of Sicily. The much-visited tourist town of Pozzuoli near Naples has a Piazza Italo Balbo. Further, a section of Ciampino Airport in Rome is named Piazzale Italo Balbo, although the tribute encountered strident opposition from politicians and activists on the left. For its part, the modern Italian air force doesn't shy away from taking ownership of Balbo, proudly acknowledging his role in its history, one that it traces not to the foundation of the Italian republic in 1946 but to the establishment of the *Regia Aeronautica* in 1923. Visitors to the Italian air force command center in Rome will encounter a life-size bronze bust of Balbo on the grounds of the complex, along with memorials to those on board the I-MANU when it was shot down. Likewise, a park in the town of Orbatello, site of the since decommissioned seaplane base, is named after the former air minister, although this, too, stirred up no small amount of controversy.

In July 2021, yet another university professor, again citing the deployment of the *Regia Aeronautica* during the 1935–36 Italo-Ethiopian War, suggested that both the column and the street name be countered with tributes honoring John C. Robinson. An African American, Robinson was a Tuskegee Airman who lent his services to the Ethiopians during the Italian invasion. Since Balbo, in his "infamy," had presumably been complicit in the *Regia Aeronautica*'s actions during the conflict, the proposed Robinson tributes would serve a sumptuous dish of poetic justice.

The spoiler here is that the professor—like Jarret, Shiller and dozens of other activists, journalists and academics—is unaware of the fact that not only did Balbo not engage in dropping bombs on Ethiopians in any way, form or capacity, but he actually opposed the 1935 invasion. In the similar manner, those from the same quarter who have and continue to depict Balbo as an Italic Himmler or Eichmann might pause to consider this summation offered by late historian and author Blaine Taylor: "Anti-German, he [Balbo] was also pro-Allied…pro-Jewish, he was therefore by definition, anti-Nazi."

Of course, the Chicago tributes have not been without their strident defenders. The late Dominic Di Frisco, who until his death in 2019 was a towering leader in Chicago's Italian American community, could always be expected to make the case for their retention. An eloquent speaker and an active Democrat, he was a familiar and much-liked figure in both city hall and Chicago's business community, and his cordial diplomacy and persuasiveness went a long way in laying calls against the removal of the column or street sign to at least temporary rest.

Di Frisco's passing represented the severing of one of the last living connections to the Decennale. He had been among the organizers of the first return visit of the *Atlantici* in 1962 and was personally acquainted with the Klein family. His was therefore able to view the tributes from a perspective no longer available to anyone today. His passion for the preservation of the tributes was such that he once vowed to chain himself to the column to prevent its removal.

It was not only the monument's retention but also its badly eroding condition that motivated Italian community activist Frank Di Piero to contact the Chicago Park District and inquire about its restoration. In a series of subsequent meetings, the idea was explored of constructing some type of shelter around it that, at least to some measure, would reduce its exposure to the punishing effects of Chicago weather and lessen future deterioration. Architectural conceptions of potential designs were drawn, but ultimately the obstacle of high expenses could not be overcome.

In the course of the conversations, Di Piero and a group of Italian Americans who had joined him in the project suggested that until the monument's ultimate fate was determined, a plaque should be placed near it with an explanation clarifying its history and significance. Both city hall and the park district were agreeable, and this author was asked to provide a text. This was submitted to then Chicago City Council chairman Ed Burke by Enza Ranieri, then president of the Joint Civic Committee of Italian Americans, but no further action was taken, leaving the discussion to be wholly eclipsed in the sociopolitical upheavals wrought by the COVID pandemic and the George Floyd incident. The proposed inscription reads:

This 2,000 year old column from the ancient Roman port of Ostia Antica, was presented to the City of Chicago by the Fascist Government of the Kingdom of Italy in 1934 in grateful recognition of our city's enthusiastic reception of the transatlantic air squadron led by General Italo Balbo of the Royal Italian Air Force on July 15th, 1933, at the Century of Progress World's Fair.

Their unprecedented formation flight from Italy to Chicago of 24 aircraft marked an important milestone in aviation and was universally celebrated for the intricate technical and logistical planning that resulted in its successful execution. The City of Chicago proudly accepted this column, which stands on the former site of the Italian Pavilion at the World's Fair, to commemorate its role in this great aeronautical achievement.

Free of any political connotations or endorsements, and as the only artifact still standing in place from the Fair, the column remains in tribute to the heroic transatlantic flyers and as a reminder of the ever-changing course of history.

BIBLIOGRAPHY

Historical Newspaper Archives: *Baltimore Sun*, *Brooklyn Daily Eagle*, *Brooklyn Times Union*, *Chicago Daily News*, *Chicago Daily Tribune*, *Chicago Examiner*, *Chicago Sun Times*, *Chicago Tribune*, *New York Daily News*, *New York Times*, *Pittsburgh Courier*, *TIME* magazine and *Washington Post*.

Balbo, Italo. *My Air Armada*. London: Hurst & Blackett, Ltd., 1934.
———. *Stormi in Volo Sull'Oceano*. Milan: Mondadori, 1931.
Cupini, Ranieri. *Cieli e Mari*. Milan: U. Mursia & C., 1973.
Doordan, Dennis P. *Italy's Contribution to the Century of Progress Exhibition*. Chicago: Prestel, 1993.
Ludovico, Domenico. *Italian Aviators from Rome to Tokyo in 1920*. Rome: Etas Kompass. 1970.
Mencarelli, Igino. *Italo Balbo*. Rome: Ufficio Storico Aeronautica Militare, 1969.
Official Book of the Flight of General Italo Balbo and His Italian Air Armada to A Century of Progress. Chicago: Cuneo Press, 1933.
Reboro, Enrico, and Paolo Gianvanni. *Pagine di Storia*. Sesto Calende, IT: Edizioni Aeronautiche Italiane, 1982.
Segre, Claudio. *Italo Balbo—A Fascist Life*. Berkeley: University of California Press, 1987.
Stone, Ellery. "Communications for the Italian Transatlantic Flight." *Journal of Electrical Communication* (August 1934).

Taylor, Blaine. *Fascist Eagle*. Missoula, MT: Pictorial Histories Publishing Company, 1996.

Ten Years of Italian Progress. Rome: Italian Tourist Information Office, 1933.

Thompson, Jonathon. *Italian Civil & Military Aircraft*. Glendale, CA: Aero Publishers, 1963.

Tycho, Charles. "Benito Mussolini Saved My Life." *Jerusalem Post*, February 27, 2020.

ABOUT THE AUTHOR

 orn in Chicago, Don Fiore has been a lifelong student of Italian history, an anti-defamation activist, a writer and a columnist on subjects of Italian and Italian American cultural and historical interest for *Fra Noi* and other local and national publications. He has been a musician and assistant manager of Caliendo's Banda Napoletana, one of the few remaining Italian-style symphonic bands in the United States, for the past five decades. In 2004, he was officially conferred the title of Cavaliere (Knight) by the president of Italy for his work promoting and preserving Italian cultural heritage.